Trauma, PTSD and Eating Disorders

This book outlines the state of the literature on the intersection between trauma exposure, PTSD, and eating disorders and provides several new research updates in this area. The functional relationship between these variables is discussed, and promising treatment approaches are provided.

It is well known that individuals with eating disorders report high rates of trauma exposure and often have co-occurring posttraumatic stress disorder (PTSD). However, most research to date has focused on the prevalence of trauma/PTSD among people with eating disorders or cross-sectional associations among these conditions. Although trauma histories and PTSD can impact eating disorder treatment and recovery, very little is known about mechanisms of these associations, which could represent important treatment targets, and few longitudinal studies have investigated these associations. Further, little research has examined trauma-focused eating disorder treatment or integrated treatment for comorbid eating disorders and PTSD. The chapters in this volume fill these critical gaps with a focus on mechanisms and treatment. They focus on new contributions to the trauma exposure/PTSD-eating disorder link, potential mediators of the association between trauma/PTSD and eating disorders, and developing effective treatments for comorbid eating disorders and PTSD. This book discusses the functional relationships between trauma, PTSD, and ED symptoms and highlights potential treatment approaches to advance this important field of research. This book will be relevant to students, professionals, and researchers in the fields of psychology, mental health, and social work.

The chapters in this book were originally published as a special issue of *Eating Disorders: The Journal of Treatment and Prevention.*

Julie G. Trim is a Clinical Psychologist who directed the Adult Eating Disorders Program at UCSD, USA. She developed and oversaw a trauma track for patients with co-occurring PTSD and eating disorders (EDs).

Karen S. Mitchell is a Clinical Research Psychologist in the National Center for PTSD and an Associate Professor of Psychiatry at the Boston University Chobanian & Avedisian School of Medicine, USA. Her program of research focuses on eating disorders, trauma, and PTSD as well as health disparities.

Kathryn Trottier is a Clinical Psychologist and Clinical Program Lead in the Eating Disorder Program at the University Health Network, Canada, and an Assistant Professor in the Department of Psychiatry at the University of Toronto, Canada. She has focused her career on delivering, developing, and evaluating evidence-based psychotherapies for eating disorders.

Trauma, PTSD and Eating Disorders

Edited by
Julie G. Trim, Karen S. Mitchell and Kathryn Trottier

Routledge
Taylor & Francis Group
LONDON AND NEW YORK

First published 2025
by Routledge
4 Park Square, Milton Park, Abingdon, Oxon, OX14 4RN

and by Routledge
605 Third Avenue, New York, NY 10158

Routledge is an imprint of the Taylor & Francis Group, an informa business

British Library Cataloguing-in-Publication Data
A catalogue record for this book is available from the British Library

ISBN13: 978-1-003-86353-3 (hbk)
ISBN13: 978-1-003-86354-0 (pbk)
ISBN13: 978-1-003-60740-3 (ebk)

DOI: 10.4324/9781003607403

Typeset in Minion Pro
by codeMantra

Publisher's Note
The publisher accepts responsibility for any inconsistencies that may have arisen during the conversion of this book from journal articles to book chapters, namely the inclusion of journal terminology.

Contents

Citation Information

The following chapters in this book were originally published in *Eating Disorders: The Journal of Treatment and Prevention*, Volume 29, issue 3 (2021). When citing this material, please use the original page numbering for each article, as follows:

Introduction

Trauma, PTSD, and eating disorders
Julie G. Trim
Eating Disorders: The Journal of Treatment and Prevention, Volume 29, issue 3 (2021), pp. 205–207

Chapter 1

Longitudinal associations of trauma exposure with disordered eating: Lessons from the Great Smoky Mountains Study
Rachel L. Zelkowitz, Noga Zerubavel, Nancy L. Zucker and William E. Copeland
Eating Disorders: The Journal of Treatment and Prevention, Volume 29, issue 3 (2021), pp. 208–225

Chapter 2

Genetic and environmental influences on posttraumatic stress disorder symptoms and disinhibited eating behaviors
Niloofar Afari, Marianna Gasperi, Cara Dochat, Jennalee S. Wooldridge, Matthew S. Herbert, Ellen A. Schur and Dedra S. Buchwald
Eating Disorders: The Journal of Treatment and Prevention, Volume 29, issue 3 (2021), pp. 226–244

Chapter 3

Intimate partner violence and muscularity-building behavior in latino sexual minority men
Alexandra D. Convertino, John P. Brady, William Grunewald and Aaron J. Blashill
Eating Disorders: The Journal of Treatment and Prevention, Volume 29, issue 3 (2021), pp. 245–259

Chapter 4

Understanding relationships between posttraumatic stress disorder symptoms, binge-eating symptoms, and obesity-related quality of life: the role of experiential avoidance
Jennalee S. Wooldridge, Matthew S. Herbert, Cara Dochat and Niloofar Afari
Eating Disorders: The Journal of Treatment and Prevention, Volume 29, issue 3 (2021), pp. 260–275

Chapter 5

Examining the roles of emotion dysregulation and impulsivity in the relationship between psychological trauma and substance abuse among women with bulimic-spectrum pathology
Lauren M. Schaefer, Vivienne M. Hazzard, Kathryn E. Smith, Cassandra A. Johnson, Li Cao, Ross D. Crosby, Carol B. Peterson, Scott J. Crow, Anna M. Bardone-Cone, Thomas E. Joiner, Daniel Le Grange, Marjorie H. Klein, James E. Mitchell and Stephen A. Wonderlich
Eating Disorders: The Journal of Treatment and Prevention, Volume 29, issue 3 (2021), pp. 276–291

Chapter 6

Posttraumatic stress disorder and eating disorders: maintaining mechanisms and treatment targets
Karen S. Mitchell, Erica R. Scioli, Tara Galovski, Perry L. Belfer and Zafra Cooper
Eating Disorders: The Journal of Treatment and Prevention, Volume 29, issue 3 (2021), pp. 292–306

Chapter 7

Integrating cognitive processing therapy for posttraumatic stress disorder with cognitive behavioral therapy for eating disorders in PROJECT RECOVER
Kathryn Trottier and Candice M. Monson
Eating Disorders: The Journal of Treatment and Prevention, Volume 29, issue 3 (2021), pp. 307–325

Notes on Contributors

Niloofar Afari, Department of Psychiatry, University of California, San Diego, USA; Department of Mental Health, Department of Research, VA San Diego Healthcare System, USA.

Anna M. Bardone-Cone, Department of Psychology, University of North Carolina, USA.

Perry L. Belfer, Newton-Wellesley Eating Disorders & Behavioral Medicine, USA; Department of Psychiatry, McLean Hospital and Harvard Medical School, Boston, USA.

Aaron J. Blashill, Department of Psychology, College of Sciences, San Diego State University, USA.

John P. Brady, San Diego State University/University of California San Diego Joint Doctoral Program in Clinical Psychology, USA.

Dedra S. Buchwald, Elson S Floyd College of Medicine, Washington State University, Spokane, USA.

Li Cao, Center for Biobehavioral Research, Sanford Research, Fargo, USA.

Alexandra D. Convertino, California State University-Dominguez Hills, Carson, USA.

Zafra Cooper, Department of Psychiatry, Yale University School of Medicine, New Haven, USA.

William E. Copeland, Department of Psychiatry, University of Vermont, Burlington, USA.

Ross D. Crosby, Center for Biobehavioral Research, Sanford Research, Fargo, USA; College of Human Medicine, Michigan State University, Flint, USA.

Scott J. Crow, Department of Psychiatry and Behavioral Sciences, University of Minnesota, Minneapolis, USA; The Emily Program, St. Paul, USA.

Cara Dochat, DBT Centre of San Diego, USA.

Tara Galovski, National Center for PTSD at VA Boston Healthcare System, USA; Boston University Chobanian & Avedisian School of Medicine, USA.

Marianna Gasperi, VA Center of Excellence for Stress and Mental Health, San Diego, USA; Department of Psychiatry, University of California, San Diego, USA; Department of Mental Health, Department of Research, VA San Diego Healthcare System, USA.

William Grunewald, Department of Psychology, College of Sciences, San Diego State University, USA.

Vivienne M. Hazzard, College of Human Medicine, Michigan State University, Flint, USA.

Matthew S. Herbert, VA Center of Excellence for Stress and Mental Health, San Diego, USA; Department of Psychiatry, University of California, San Diego, USA; Department of Mental Health, Department of Research, VA San Diego Healthcare System, USA.

Cassandra A. Johnson, Center for Biobehavioral Research, Sanford Research, Fargo, USA; Department of Biostatistics, University of Minnesota, Minneapolis, USA.

Thomas E. Joiner, Department of Psychology, Florida State University, Tallahassee, USA.

Marjorie H. Klein, Department of Psychiatry, University of Wisconsin – Madison, USA.

Daniel Le Grange, Department of Psychiatry, University of California, San Francisco, USA.

James E. Mitchell, Center for Biobehavioral Research, Sanford Research, Fargo, USA.

Karen S. Mitchell, National Center for PTSD at VA Boston Healthcare System, USA; Boston University Chobanian & Avedisian School of Medicine, USA.

Candice M. Monson, Centre for Mental Health, Ryerson University, Toronto, Canada.

Carol B. Peterson, Department of Psychiatry and Behavioral Sciences, University of Minnesota, Minneapolis, USA; The Emily Program, St. Paul, USA.

Lauren M. Schaefer, Center for Biobehavioral Research, Sanford Research, Fargo, USA.

Ellen A. Schure, Department of Medicine, University of Washington, Seattle, USA.

Erica R. Scioli, National Center for PTSD at VA Boston Healthcare System, USA; Boston University Chobanian & Avedisian School of Medicine, USA.

Kathryn E. Smith, Center for Biobehavioral Research, Sanford Research, Fargo, USA; Department of Psychiatry and Behavioral Science, School of Medicine and Health Sciences, University of North Dakota, Fargo, USA.

Julie G. Trim, Department of Psychiatry, University of California San Diego, San Diego, California, USA

Kathryn Trottier, Centre for Mental Health, University Health Network, Toronto, Canada; Department of Psychiatry, University of Toronto, Canada.

Stephen A. Wonderlich, Center for Biobehavioral Research, Sanford Research, Fargo, USA; College of Human Medicine, Michigan State University, Flint, USA.

Jennalee S. Wooldridge, VA Center of Excellence for Stress and Mental Health, San Diego, USA; Department of Psychiatry, University of California, San Diego, USA; Department of Mental Health, Department of Research, VA San Diego Healthcare System, USA.

Rachel L. Zelkowitz, Women's Health Sciences Division, National Center for PTSD, VA Boston Healthcare System, Boston University Chobanian & Avedisian School of Medicine, USA.

Noga Zerubavel, Department of Psychiatry and Behavioral Sciences, Duke University Medical Center, Durham, USA.

Nancy L. Zucker, Department of Psychiatry and Behavioral Sciences, Duke University Medical Center, Durham, USA; Department of Psychology and Neuroscience, Duke University, Durham, USA.

Introduction: trauma, PTSD, and eating disorders

Julie G. Trim

To date, a plethora of scientific studies have examined the relationship between psychological trauma or posttraumatic stress disorder (PTSD) and eating disorders (EDs). However, the literature thus far has focused largely on prevalence estimates, descriptive statistics, and correlational data. There have been relatively few studies on mechanisms of the PTSD-ED association, particularly longitudinal ones. Further, trauma and PTSD often complicate the course of ED treatment and make it more difficult for individuals with this comorbidity to achieve a full recovery (Keel & Brown, 2010; Trottier, 2020), underscoring the need for more research on integrated treatments. While the clinical implications of comorbid PTSD and ED are clear, there are still substantial gaps in the literature that necessitate further exploration.

As scientist-practitioners, we felt an urgency to push the literature forward and thus decided to compile a special issue on this topic. In our call for papers, we noted specific interest in two types of manuscripts: 1) studies that tackled complex questions about the functional relationship between trauma or PTSD, and ED symptoms, and 2) treatment-focused studies based on sound theoretical rationale or preliminary empirical support. Fortunately, we received several articles that met these criteria, and believe that the resulting special issue represents a meaningful contribution to the literature.

This special issue is divided into three sections, with each section focusing on a specific theme. Part 1, "New Contributions to the Trauma Exposure/PTSD-ED link" features three articles examining the relationship between trauma exposure or PTSD, and ED symptomatology. The section begins with an article by Zelkowitz et al. (2021) that explores cross-sectional and longitudinal effects of various forms of trauma exposure (violent, sexual, and other) and PTSD on disordered eating among 1,420 community-based youth. Next, Afari et al. (2021) examine the genetic and environmental relationships between PTSD symptoms and maladaptive eating behaviors in a community sample of 400 same-sex twins. Finally, Convertino et al. (2021) explore the association between two correlates of ED behavior among Latino men who have sex with men (MSM)—muscularity-related dissatisfaction and muscularity-oriented behavior—and a specific type of trauma exposure, interpersonal violence (IPV).

Part II, "Mechanisms of Effect," consists of two articles that examine potential mediators of the relationship between trauma or PTSD, and ED symptomatology. The first article explores experiential avoidance as a putative mediator of the relationship between PTSD and binge-eating symptoms, as well as PTSD and obesity-related quality of life (Wooldridge et al., 2021). In the second article, Schaefer et al. (2021) examine emotion dysregulation and impulsivity as possible mediators of the relationship between distinct forms of childhood trauma and the presence of problematic alcohol/drug use among women with bulimic-spectrum pathology.

Part III, "Developing Effective ED-PTSD Treatments" presents promising treatment considerations and approaches for individuals with comorbid ED and PTSD symptoms. The first article by Mitchell et al. (2021) presents an integrated cognitive-behavioral theory elucidating the bidirectional relationship of EDs and PTSD, and subsequently proposes important treatment targets for this subpopulation. Trottier and Monson (2021) then outline two integrated ED-PTSD treatment approaches with good preliminary empirical support: (1) Cognitive Processing Therapy (CPT) for individuals in ED treatment (Trottier & Monson, 2014), and (2) manualized, individual cognitive-behavioral therapy addressing both ED and PTSD (Integrated CBT for ED-PTSD; Trottier & Monson, 2014) after initial ED stabilization.

Conclusion

Research on the intersections of trauma, PTSD, and ED symptomatology has grown steadily over the past few decades. Nonetheless, our scientific knowledge in this area is in broad "brushstrokes" as opposed to nuanced understanding. Our goals in publishing this special issue were to better elucidate the functional relationships between trauma, PTSD, and ED symptoms, and to disseminate promising treatment approaches to clinicians working with this population. The collection of articles in this special issue advance the literature in several ways: 1) comparing cross-sectional and longitudinal data on trauma, PTSD, and disordered eating, 2) comparing the relative associations of trauma type (e.g., physical abuse) and disordered eating, 3) identifying genetic overlap between PTSD and maladaptive eating behaviors, 4) exploring the impact of a specific type of trauma on ED symptoms in an understudied population, 5) testing potential mediators of the link between trauma/PTSD and EDs, 6) proposing a comprehensive model of the bidirectional relationship between PTSD and EDs based on cognitive behavioral theory, and 7) describing two approaches to treatment with promising results.

Ongoing research on this topic is still needed. While the articles in this special issue help elucidate the relationship between trauma, PTSD, and EDs, moderators and mediators need to be identified and additional longitudinal data needs to be collected to parse out effects over time. Moreover, Trottier et al.'s (2017) article surveying "frontline" ED clinicians suggests that clinicians see the importance of treating PTSD in our ED clients, but desperately need guidance on how to effectively treat their clients. We urge clinicians and researchers to design, implement, and publish data on integrated treatments for this subpopulation so best practices can be identified.

References

Afari, N., Gasperi, M., Cara, D., Wooldridge J.S., Herbert, M.S., Schur, E., Buchwald, D. (2021). Genetic and Environmental Influences on Posttraumatic Stress Disorder Symptoms and Disinhibited Eating Behaviors. Eating Disorders, 29(3), (226–244). 10.1080/10640266.2020.1864587

Convertino, A.D., Brady, J.P., Grunewald, W., Blashill, A., (2021). Intimate Partner Violence and Muscularity-Building Behavior in Latino Sexual Minority Men. Eating Disorders, 29(3), (245–259). 10.1080/10640266.2021.1891371

Keel, P. K., & Brown, T. A. (2010). Update on course and outcome in eating disorders. *International Journal of Eating Disorders*, *43*(3), 195–204. https://doi.org/10.1002/eat.20810

Schaefer, L.M., Hazzard, V.M., Smith, K., Johnson, C.A., Cao, L., Crosby, R., Peterson, C,B., Crow, S.J., Bardone-Cone, A.M., Joiner, T.E., Le Grange, D., Klein, M.H., Mitchell, J.E., Wonderlich, S. (2021). Examining the roles of emotion dysregulation and impulsivity in the relationship between psychological trauma and substance abuse among women with bulimic-spectrum pathology. Eating Disorders, 29(3), (276–291). 10.1080/10640266.2021.1891370

Trottier, K. (2020). Posttraumatic stress disorder predicts non-completion of day hospital treatment for bulimia nervosa and other specified feeding/eating disorder. European Eating Disorders Review, 28(3), 343–350. https://doi.org/10.1002/erv.2723

Trottier, K., & Monson, C. M. (2014). *Integrated cognitive behavioral therapy for co-occurring eating disorder and posttraumatic stress disorder.* [Unpublished manual].

Trottier, K., Monson, C. M., Wonderlich, S. A., MacDonald, D. E., & Olmsted, M. P. (2017). Frontline clinicians' perspectives on and utilization of trauma-focused therapy with individuals with eating disorders. *Eating Disorders*, *25*(1), 22–36. https://doi.org/10.1080/10640266.2016.1207456

Trottier, K., Monson, C.M., (2021). Integrating Cognitive Processing Therapy for Posttraumatic Stress Disorder with Cognitive Behavioral Therapy for Eating Disorders in PROJECT RECOVER. Eating Disorders, 29(3), (307–325). 10.1080/10640266.2021.1891372

Wooldridge, J.S., Herbert, M.S., Dochat, C., Afari, N., (2021). Understanding Relationships Between Posttraumatic Stress Disorder Symptoms, Binge-Eating Symptoms, and Obesity-Related Quality of Life: The Role of Experiential Avoidance. Eating Disorders, 29(3), (260–275). 10.1080/10640266.2020.1868062

Zelkowitz, R., Noga, Z., Nancy, Z., William, E.Z. (2021). Longitudinal Associations of Trauma Exposure with Disordered Eating: Lessons from the Great Smoky Mountains Study. Eating Disorders, 29(3), (208–225). 10.1080/10640266.2021.1921326

Part I

New contributions to the trauma exposure/PTSD-ED link

Longitudinal associations of trauma exposure with disordered eating: lessons from the Great Smoky Mountains Study

Rachel L. Zelkowitz, Noga Zerubavel, Nancy L. Zucker, and William E. Copeland

ABSTRACT

Disordered eating is prevalent among trauma survivors, yet little is known about mechanisms underlying this relation. We explored cross-sectional and longitudinal associations of trauma exposure and posttraumatic stress disorder symptoms (PTSD) with disordered eating among 1,420 community-based youth participating in the Great Smoky Mountain Study. Participants were interviewed about trauma exposure, PTSD symptoms, and disordered eating at regular intervals throughout childhood, adolescence, and early adulthood. Our findings confirmed associations of all forms of trauma exposure (violent, sexual, and other) with disordered eating symptoms in childhood and adulthood, although the pattern of results varied by disordered eating symptom and trauma exposure type. Only non-sexual, non-violent trauma exposure in childhood had significant associations with any disordered eating symptoms in adulthood. Within childhood, trauma exposures but not PTSD symptoms showed significant longitudinal associations with bulimia nervosa symptoms and sustained appetite changes and preoccupation with eating. In adulthood, PTSD symptoms but not trauma exposures showed significant longitudinal associations only with bulimia nervosa symptoms. The association of specific PTSD clusters on bulimia nervosa symptoms was significant for reexperiencing, whereas hyperarousal symptoms trended toward significance. The impact of trauma exposures on disordered eating may vary by developmental period.

Clinical implications

- Age-related differences emerged between trauma and disordered eating.
- Both sexual and non-sexual traumas were linked to childhood disordered eating.

- Posttraumatic stress disorder symptoms did not predict childhood disordered eating.
- Posttraumatic stress disorder symptoms predicted adult bulimia nervosa symptoms.
- Reexperiencing symptoms specifically predicted adult bulimia nervosa symptoms.

Introduction

Disordered eating (DE) is highly prevalent among those who have been exposed to trauma, but we know relatively little about the mechanisms underlying this relation (Brewerton, 2007). DE refers to aberrant eating and weight-control behaviors (e.g., food restriction, binge eating, purging and other inappropriate compensatory methods) that may or may not occur in the context of a clinically diagnosable eating disorder. Research on the association of trauma exposure and DE has largely relied on retrospective data and focused on traumatic experiences and diagnostic status of posttraumatic stress disorder (PTSD) rather than specific PTSD symptoms. Thus, longitudinal studies that explore how trauma exposure influences vulnerability for subsequent DE and the possible mechanisms by which this occurs would provide vital information for the development of targeted prevention and intervention programs.

Although clinically diagnosable eating disorders are relatively rare in the general population (among adolescents, 0.3% and 0.9% lifetime prevalence for anorexia nervosa and bulimia nervosa; Swanson et al., 2011), DE is more common than such full-threshold disorders (Solmi et al., 2015). For example, the past-year prevalence of self-induced vomiting among 16-year-old girls ranged from 33.5% to 9.7%across three adolescent cohort studies (N = 7,418; Solmi et al., 2015). Restrictive eating (e.g., fasting, skipping meals) was reported by 60.7% of high-school girls and 27.9% of high-school boys in the Project of Eating and Activity in Teens and Young Adults; Neumark-Sztainer et al., 2011). DE has been linked to impairments in physical and psychological functioning (Lipson & Sonneville, 2020; Solmi et al., 2015; Stice & Bearman, 2001). Given this, studying vulnerability factors for DE may be of particular importance. The current study examined the longitudinal associations of trauma exposure with DE in childhood and adulthood using data from a 16-year, population-based cohort study. We also examined the associations of specific PTSD symptom clusters with DE in adulthood.

Cross-sectional associations of trauma and DE

Research on trauma exposure and DE initially focused on childhood maltreatment, especially childhood sexual abuse (e.g., Smolak & Murnen, 2002). Recent meta-analyses provided evidence for associations between multiple types of childhood maltreatment with eating disorders (Caslini et al., 2016; Molendijk et al., 2017; Pignatelli et al., 2017). Molendijk et al. (2017) further found associations between childhood maltreatment with eating disorder severity and psychiatric comorbidity. Other forms of trauma exposure have also been linked to DE (e.g., physical and sexual assault, motor vehicle accidents, bullying; Copeland, Bulik et al., 2015; Dansky et al., 1997; Mitchell et al., 2012). Although these studies provide important foundational knowledge about the connection between trauma exposures and DE, they have largely been limited by cross-sectional designs and retrospective recall of trauma histories (Trottier & MacDonald, 2017).

Longitudinal associations between trauma and DE

Prospective analyses of trauma exposure and DE are limited. In the first longitudinal cohort study of trauma and DE, Johnson et al. (2002) analyzed the association of childhood trauma and subsequent DE among a sample of youth from upstate New York. Childhood sexual abuse and physical neglect predicted an eating disorder diagnosis or endorsing purging or strict dieting in adolescence or young adulthood, even after controlling for childhood DE. Other studies have combined prospective assessments of DE with retrospective reports of childhood trauma. For example, Sanci et al. (2008) prospectively assessed DE symptoms throughout adolescence in a cohort of Australian youth and later asked participants if they had experienced sexual abuse during childhood (i.e., prior to designated assessments of DE). Results showed that exposure to two or more episodes of childhood sexual abuse was associated with later onset of bulimia nervosa (BN) symptoms among girls. In a longitudinal assessment of the effects of combat exposure, Jacobson et al. (2008) found that this trauma exposure predicted the onset of DE among women military personnel. Taken together, these studies suggest multiple forms of trauma exposure may precede DE, but further research in diverse samples is needed to confirm these relations.

Associations of PTSD symptoms with DE

Parsing the effects of trauma exposure from PTSD symptoms on DE represents an important step for the field (e.g., Brewerton, 2007; Trottier & MacDonald, 2017; Trottier et al., 2016). PTSD symptoms have been found to predict subsequent binge eating among various adult populations (e.g., community samples, military personnel, women who identify as sexual minorities; Cronce et al., 2017; Mason et al., 2017; Mitchell et al., 2016). There is growing evidence for PTSD symptoms as a mediator of trauma exposure and DE, although much of this is based on cross-sectional data (Dubosc et al., 2012; Holzer et al., 2008; Huston et al., 2019).

It is unclear how or whether specific symptoms of PTSD relate differentially to DE. Trottier et al. (2016) proposed that DE may function to facilitate avoidance of trauma-related affect and cognitions or downregulate negative arousal among people with PTSD. They note that the behaviors may also stem from negative self-focused cognitions and affect associated with PTSD; others have hypothesized that disordered eating may reflect body-focused shame or responses to negative cognitions about control or safety among trauma survivors (Trim et al., 2017). A network analysis of PTSD symptoms and DE identified heightened connectivity across several constructs: irritability and binge eating, nightmares and body dissatisfaction, and concentration difficulties associated with PTSD symptoms and concentration difficulties linked with distress over shape and weight (Vanzhula et al., 2019). The authors suggested that binge eating may function to regulate irritability (or provoke irritability), whereas nightmares related to trauma experiences may increase body dissatisfaction if individuals ruminate on the potential role of body shape and size in their victimization. Substantial work remains to confirm these interpretations and clarify associations both cross-sectionally and over time, however.

Current study

Although researchers have noted associations of trauma exposures (especially childhood maltreatment) with DE, there are limited examples of longitudinal studies that prospectively examine a range of trauma exposures, PTSD, and DE symptoms. Further, much of the extant literature has relied on retrospective recall of trauma exposures and DE symptoms. Prospective assessment of trauma exposure, PTSD symptoms, and DE is thus critical to clarifying the role of trauma exposure and PTSD symptoms in subsequent DE.

Accordingly, we had had three main aims in the current study. First, we sought to confirm previous research on the association of trauma exposure and DE symptoms by evaluating their associations within childhood and adulthood in a single cohort. We focused on DE symptoms rather than clinical eating disorders due to the greater prevalence of the former in both our sample and the general population. We hypothesized that DE symptoms would be heightened among those exposed to sexual or violent trauma in comparison to no trauma exposure, given extensive evidence for cross-sectional associations of such trauma exposures and DE in the literature. Second, we sought to assess the longitudinal association of trauma exposure with DE. We did this both across age groups (i.e., testing the association of childhood trauma exposure with adulthood DE after controlling for childhood DE) and within age group (i.e., using trauma exposure at one observation to predict DE symptoms at the next observation within childhood and adulthood periods). We hypothesized that sexual or violent trauma exposures in childhood would each significantly relate to DE in adulthood after controlling for baseline DE. We also hypothesized that exposure to sexual or violent trauma at one wave would significantly relate to increased DE symptoms at the following wave during both developmental periods. Finally, we evaluated the association of PTSD symptoms (examined in total and by symptom cluster) with subsequent DE. We anticipated significant associations of PTSD with DE but had no a priori hypotheses about the associations of each PTSD symptom cluster on DE symptoms.

Methods

Participants

Participants included individuals (n = 1420, 51.1% female) recruited as part of the Great Smoky Mountain Study, a population-based longitudinal cohort study examining trajectories of emotional and behavioral concerns from youth to adulthood (Costello, 1996). The study began in 1992 and continues today. The screening and recruitment process are described in detail in Costello (1996) and Costello et al. (2016). Briefly, a sample of 4,500 youth enrolled in public schools across 11 counties in western North Carolina was randomly selected to participate in an initial eligibility screening. Children whose parents or caregivers reported heightened levels of behavioral concerns were invited to participate in the full study. Ten percent of children who scored below this threshold were also randomly selected to participate in the study. Additionally, all American Indian youth attending reservation schools in the Qualla Boundary in North Carolina (n = 450) were invited to participate. At baseline, the sample was 64.51% Caucasian, 5.56% African American, 0.21% Asian American, 0.42% Hispanic, and 22.75% American Indian. Less than o1%of the sample identified as more than one race (Costello, 1996). Over the course of childhood, approximately one-third of participants lived below the federal poverty line during at least one assessment (Copeland, Wolke et al., 2015).

Procedures

Participants were recruited in 1993 at ages 9 (n = 508), 11 (n = 497), or 13 (n = 415). Trained study personnel interviewed both the youth and their parents at baseline and annually for f4 years(i.e., until the oldest participants were 16). The participants were then interviewed alone at ages 19, 21, 25, and 30. They

Table 1. Frequency of trauma exposures and disordered eating symptoms reported in childhood, through adulthood.

Trauma Exposure			
Category	Example exposures	Childhood Frequency[1] (*N*, %)	Cumulative Lifetime Frequency[1] (*N*, %)
Any	Any form of trauma exposure	1007 (67.7)	1222 (86.1)
Sexual	Rape, sexual abuse	184 (11.0)	313(20.6)
Violent	Physical abuse, violent death of loved one, experiencing physical violence, war or terrorism, captivity	419 (25.0)	692 (45.4)
Other	Witnessing trauma with potential to cause death or injury, learning about a loved one's trauma exposure, natural disaster, fire, serious unintentional injury, diagnosis of serious illness, exposure to noxious agent	840 (56.5)	1074 (75.8)
Frequency of Eating Disorder Symptoms			
Category	Definition	Childhood Frequency (*N*, %)	Cumulative Lifetime Frequency (*N*, %)
Any AN symptom	Endorsed any of the following: • Underweight • Fear of gaining weight • Distorted body image	274 (19.7)	375 (26.5)
Any BN symptom	Endorsed any of the following: • Binge eating • Any attempts to reduce weight (via self-induced vomiting, dieting, excessive exercise) • Overconcern with body image	673 (42.2)	792 (50.4)
Any Associated DE symptom	Endorsed any of the following: • Sustained increased appetite • Sustained decreased appetite • Preoccupation with food/eating	966 (69.8)	1096 (78.5)

Note. All *N*s are unweighted. Categories are consistent with those outlined in Copeland et al. (2015). [1]Dichotomous variable based on whether participants reported exposure at any available observation during the time period.

completed 11,084 interviews over the course of the study, with at least 76% of pthe participantscompleting interviews at any given assessment (Costello et al., 2016). Childhood trauma exposure was unrelated to dropout during adulthood (Copeland et al., 2018). All interviews were audiotaped, and interviewers participated in regular reviews of randomly selected tapes to ensure fidelity. The study protocol and consent forms for each assessment were approved by the Duke University Medical Center Institutional Review Board, and participants received payment for their time.

Measures

Disordered eating

Participants were interviewed using the Child and Adolescent Psychiatric Assessment (CAPA; Angold et al., 1995) until age 16, followed by a version adapted for young adults (the Young Adult Psychiatric Assessment, YAPA; Angold & Costello, 2000). Parents were interviewed about their child's symptoms until the child was 16. Evaluation of the CAPA by multiple indices (e.g., prevalence of detected diagnoses, association with expected outcomes, etc.) supports the test–retest reliability and constructs validity of the instrument (Angold & Costello, 2000; Copeland, Wolke et al., 2015). DE items remained the same across both measures, although the YAPA was not separately validated. Participants reported on eating behaviors and body image concerns over the 3 months prior to each observation. The instruments specifically assessed for the presence of each symptom of anorexia nervosa (AN) and bulimia nervosa (BN) in the Diagnostic and Statistical Manual of Mental Disorders-IV (DSM-IV; American Psychiatric Association, 2000). We used clusters described in (Copeland, Bulik et al., 2015): AN symptoms, BN symptoms, and associated disordered eating (i.e., preoccupation with eating, sustained increased/decreased appetite). See Table 1 for items pertaining to each cluster. Items were coded as present if endorsed by either the youth or their parent. We examined each of these clusters separately throughout the analyses. AN items can be recoded to correspond to DSM-5 symptoms. In childhood, 0.1% of the participants met DSM-5 criteria for AN (0.6% through adulthood). Substantially greater proportions of participants endorsed DE symptoms.

Trauma exposure and posttraumatic stress disorder

The CAPA/YAPA and parent interviews assessed for a range of traumas (e.g., exposure to actual or threatened death, severe injury, or sexual violence). Youth and parents were interviewed about the youth's lifetime and recent (i.e., past t3 months trauma history at each assessment through age 16; thereafter, participants were asked about past three-month trauma exposure as well as any exposure since last assessment. We characterized trauma exposure using categories defined by Copeland et al. (2018): violent (e.g., death of a loved one through violent means, physical abuse), sexual (e.g., rape, sexual abuse; violent sexual assaults were also categorized as sexual trauma), and non-sexual, non-violent (e.g., natural disaster).

Until age 16, the full PTSD module was only completed if the parent or child reported the presence of each PTSD symptom cluster (reexperiencing, hyperarousal, and avoidance) as assessed with three screening questions. This was done to minimize response burden. Due to concern that the screening questions might have been overly restrictive, at ages 19 and 21, the PTSD module was completed if the participants reported exposure to events that involved significant threat to themselves or others. The original screening structure (three screening questions assessing reexperiencing, hyperarousal, and avoidance) was re-adopted at ages 25 and 30.

Data analytic plan

We accounted for the stratified sampling design by applying sampling weights throughout the analyses; weights were inversely proportional to a participant's chances of selection. To assess the association of trauma exposure and DE symptoms in childhood and adulthood (Aim 1), we first summed each type of trauma exposure across the childhood observations (i.e., through age 16) and adulthood observations (i.e., ages 19, 21, 25 and 30). This generated a cumulative record of each form of trauma exposure during these periods. See Table 1 for full definitions of each trauma exposure and childhood and cumulative lifetime prevalence.

We used a two-step process to calculate the DE scores used in Aim 1. First, we dichotomized whether the participant endorsed each of the items assessed in a DE symptom cluster at each observation. For example, the AN cluster encompassed three items (see Table 1); AN scores at the observation level ranged from 0 to 3. We then formed an aggregate score across childhood observations by summing the number of items within that DE symptom cluster endorsed at any observation through age 16. Items endorsed at more than one observation were only counted once, consistent with other analyses based on GSMS data (e.g., Copeland, Wolke et al., 2015). Aggregate AN scores across childhood observations thus also ranged from 0 to 3. We repeated the process for aggregating across adult observations (i.e., ages 19, 21, 25, and 30). We used the same procedure to calculate scores for BN symptoms in childhood and adulthood (both observation-level and aggregate scores ranged from 0 to 3) and associated DE symptoms (observation-level and aggregated scores again ranged from 0 to 3). We computed mean ratios for each DE symptom cluster in childhood and adulthood, comparing scores for those exposed to each type of trauma versus those with no trauma exposure.

Aim 2 was to assess the longitudinal associations of trauma exposure with DE across and within developmental periods. To assess associations across

Table 2. Associations of trauma exposure and DE symptoms by age group and trauma type.

	No trauma *M* (*SD*)	Any Trauma *M* (*SD*)	MR (95% CI)	Sexual Trauma *M* (*SD*)	MR (95% CI)	Violent Trauma *M* (*SD*)	MR(95% CI)	Other Trauma Exposure *M* (*SD*)	MR (95% CI)
Childhood Trauma with Childhood DE Symptoms									
Mean AN sx	0.12 (0.36)	0.25 (0.50)	1.9** (1.2–3.0)	0.40 (0.59)	2.3** (1.3–4.0)	0.26 (0.48)	2.0* (1.2–3.5)	0.26 (0.50)	1.9** (1.2–3.0)
Mean BN sx	0.35 (0.59)	0.58 (0.72)	1.7*** (1.3–2.2)	0.69 (0.71)	1.6** (1.1–2.3)	0.63 (0.63)	1.8*** (1.3–2.4)	0.60 (0.69)	1.7*** (1.3–2.2)
Mean Associated sx	0.61 (0.57)	0.84 (0.54)	1.4*** (1.2–1.6)	0.78 (0.58)	1.4** (1.1–1.9)	0.80 (0.51)	1.4** (1.1–1.6)	0.85 (0.53)	1.4*** (1.2–1.6)
Cumulative Lifetime Trauma with Adulthood DE Symptoms[1]									
Mean AN sx	0.10 (0.30)	0.18 (0.50)	1.6 (0.9–2.7)	0.34 (0.69)	1.9 (0.9–3.9)	0.23 (0.54)	1.9* (1.0–3.5)	0.16 (0.47)	1.4 (0.8–2.5)
Mean BN sx	0.20 (0.43)	0.39 (0.61)	1.8** (1.2–2.6)	0.58 (0.72)	1.9 (1.2–2.9)**	0.36 (0.58)	1.7** (1.1–2.5)	0.40 (0.62)	1.8** (1.3–2.8)
Mean Associated sx.	0.28 (0.45)	0.44 (0.55)	1.5** (1.1–2.0)	0.64 (0.56)	1.8*** (1.3–2.7)	0.52 (0.58)	1.7*** (1.3–2.4)	0.46 (0.56)	1.5** (1.1–2.0)

Note. AN = Anorexia nervosa, Associated symptoms = Sustained appetite change, preoccupation with food/eating, BN = Bulimia nervosa, DE = Disordered eating, MR = Mean ratio, Sx = Symptoms. Values adjusted for sex, race, and family SES. Reference group for all analyses is no trauma. [1]Dichotomous variable based on reported exposure at any available observation.
$^{*}p < .05$, $^{**}p \leq .01$, $^{***}p < .001$.

Table 3. Association of childhood trauma exposure with adult DE symptoms, by trauma type.

	No trauma*M* (*SD*)	Any Trauma *M* (*SD*)	MR (95% CI)	Sexual Trauma *M* (*SD*)	MR (95% CI)	Violent Trauma *M* (*SD*)	MR(95% CI)	Other Trauma Exposure *M* (*SD*)	MR (95% CI)
Mean AN sx	0.15 (0.40)	0.17 (0.46)	1.1 (0.7–1.9)	0.16 (0.34)	0.8 (0.4–1.7)	0.19 (0.48)	1.2 (0.6–2.5)	0.16 (0.45)	1.1 (0.6–1.9)
Mean BN sx	0.29 (0.57)	0.35 (0.56)	1.3 (0.9–1.7)	0.41 (0.55)	1.2 (0.8–1.8)	0.34 (0.49)	1.2 (0.8–1.7)	0.35 (0.56)	1.2 (0.9–1.7)
Mean Assoc. sx	0.31 (0.53)	0.43 (0.52)	1.4* (1.0–1.8)	0.41 (0.49)	1.1 (0.8–1.6)	0.43 (0.49)	1.3† (1.0–1.8)	0.44 (0.53)	1.4* (1.0–1.9)

Note. AN = Anorexia nervosa, Associated symptoms = Sustained appetite change, preoccupation with food/eating, BN = Bulimia nervosa, DE = Disordered eating, MR = Mean ratio, Sx = Symptoms. Values adjusted for sex, race, and family SES. Reference group for all analyses is no trauma.

†$p = .05$, *$p < .05$

Table 4. Longitudinal association of trauma exposure with disordered eating symptoms across waves, by trauma type and developmental period.

	Cumulative Trauma MR	95% CI	Sexual Trauma MR	95% CI	Violent Trauma MR	95% CI	Other Trauma Exposure MR	95% CI
Childhood DE								
AN sx	1.1	0.9–1.3	1.0	0.6–1.6	1.4	0.8–2.3	1.0	0.7–1.4
BN sx	1.1	1.0–1.2	1.4†	1.0–1.8	1.4**	1.1–1.7	0.9	0.7–1.1
Associated sx	1.1**	1.0–1.2	0.9	0.7–1.3	1.3*	1.0–1.6	1.2*	1.0–1.3
Adulthood DE								
AN sx	1.0	0.7–1.6	0.5	0.2–1.7	0.7	0.3–1.6	1.1	0.7–1.8
BN sx	1.1	0.9–1.3	0.9	0.5–1.6	1.1	0.7–1.6	1.1	0.8–1.5
Associated sx.	1.1	0.9–1.3	0.9	0.7–1.3	0.9	0.6–1.3	1.2	0.9–1.6

Note. AN = Anorexia nervosa, Associated symptoms = Sustained appetite change, preoccupation with food/eating, BN = Bulimia nervosa,
DE = Disordered eating, MR = Mean ratio, Sx = Symptoms. Values adjusted for DE symptoms at previous observation, sex, race, and family SES. Reference group for all analyses is no trauma.
$^{\dagger}p = .05$, $^{*}p < .05$, $^{**}p \leq .01$

Table 5. Longitudinal associations of DSM-IV PTSD symptoms with DE in adulthood.

	Any PTSD Sx		Painful Recall		Avoidance		Hyperarousal	
	MR	95% CI	MR	95% CI	MR	95% CI	MR	95% CI
AN sx	1.0	0.7–1.3	1.0	0.5–1.8	1.1	0.4–2.8	1.0	0.5–2.0
BN sx	1.1*	1.0–1.2	1.2*	1.0–1.5	1.3	0.9–2.0	1.3†	1.0–1.6
Associated sx.	1.0	0.9–1.2	1.0	0.8–1.3	1.2	0.7–1.8	1.0	0.8–1.4

Note. AN = Anorexia nervosa, Associated symptoms = Sustained appetite change, preoccupation with food/eating, BN = Bulimia nervosa,
DE = Disordered eating, MR = Mean ratio, PTSD = Posttraumatic stress disorder, Sx = Symptoms. Values adjusted for DE symptoms at previous wave, sex, race, and family SES.
$^{\dagger}p = .05$, $^{*}p < .05$.

developmental period, we regressed the aggregated scores for each DE cluster in adulthood on childhood trauma exposure. We examined each form of childhood trauma exposure in a different model. All models were adjusted for sex, race, childhood SES, and the aggregated score for the same DE symptom cluster in childhood.

We then used generalized estimating equations (GEE) with robust variance (sandwich) estimators to assess the associations of trauma exposure at one observation in childhood with the total score for each DE symptom cluster at the next observation (through age 16). As AN, BN, and associated DE symptoms were highly right-skewed, we used the Poisson distribution to account for their non-normality. We repeated this process for the adulthood assessments, using trauma exposure recorded at age 19 to predict DE symptoms at age 21, etc. Models controlled for DE symptoms at the preceding observation as well as sex, race, and childhood socioeconomic status (SES).

Aim 3 was to explore the incremental utility of specific PTSD symptom clusters on subsequent DE. We first used GEE with robust variance estimates to examine the association of endorsing any PTSD symptoms (versus no symptoms) with later DE, as we could conduct this analysis in both developmental periods by using childhood responses to the symptom cluster screening questions. We then focused on adult observations to test the association of each PTSD symptom cluster (i.e., painful recall, avoidance, hyperarousal) with DE at the next observation, controlling for DE at the reference wave, sex, race/ethnicity, and SES.

All analyses were conducted in SAS; regression models for Aims 2 and 3 were implemented using PROC GENMOD.

Results

Aim 1: assess associations between trauma and DE in childhood and adulthood

The top section of Table 2 shows mean childhood DE symptoms by trauma type, along with the association of trauma exposure with DE, adjusted for sex, race/ethnicity, and SES. All associations are shown as mean ratios, with no trauma exposure as the reference group. Unexpectedly, each form of trauma exposure in childhood was associated with increased DE symptoms during childhood. The bottom of Table 2 shows the associations between lifetime trauma exposures and DE symptoms in adulthood, adjusted for sex, race/ethnicity, and SES. As compared to those with no trauma exposure, participants reporting any lifetime violent trauma exposure reported significantly higher levels of each DE outcome in adulthood. Both exposures to lifetime sexual trauma and non-violent, non-sexual trauma were associated with higher levels of BN symptoms, appetite changes and preoccupation with food in adulthood.

Aim 2: assess longitudinal associations of trauma with DE

Table 3 shows the longitudinal association of childhood trauma exposure with DE symptoms in adulthood, controlling for sex, race, SES, and childhood DE. Any childhood trauma exposure was linked to increased appetite changes and preoccupation with food in adulthood. Of the specific categories of trauma exposure, however, only non-sexual, non-violent childhood trauma had significant longitudinal associations with adulthood DE symptoms (although violent trauma exposure trended toward significance).

Table 4 shows the associations of exposure to each form of trauma with DE symptoms at the following observation within childhood and adulthood. Analyses were adjusted for DE symptoms at the previous observation, along with sex, race, and SES. The top section shows relations across observations within childhood; the bottom section shows relations across adulthood observations Violent trauma exposure had significant longitudinal associations with BN symptoms and associated DE at the next wave in childhood (versus no trauma). Non-sexual, non-violent trauma exposure also showed a significant longitudinal association with associated DE symptoms in childhood. The association of sexual trauma trended toward significance for childhood BN symptoms. Unexpectedly, no type of adult trauma exposure had significant associations with any subsequent DE symptom in adulthood.

Aim 3: assess longitudinal associations of PTSD symptoms on DE

Across childhood observations, endorsing any PTSD symptom was not significantly related to any form of DE at the subsequent wave after controlling for DE at the prior observation, sex, race, and SES. Due to the low prevalence of PTSD symptoms in childhood, we could not parse associations of specific PTSD symptom clusters on DE during this period.

Across adulthood observations, endorsing any PTSD symptom was significantly associated with increased BN symptoms at the subsequent wave, again controlling for previous DE, sex, race/ethnicity, and SES. (See Table 5). . When we examined each cluster individually, only associations with painful recall were significant. The association with hyperarousal trended toward significance. PTSD symptoms had no significant longitudinal associations with symptoms of AN or associated DE.

Discussion

The unique attributes of the Great Smoky Mountain Study allowed for prospective assessment of trauma exposure on subsequent DE, extending a literature that has largely focused on cross-sectional associations of these constructs. In the current study, we aimed to confirm previously documented associations of different trauma exposures with DE in a large community-based sample, as well examine the longitudinal associations of trauma exposure and PTSD specifically with DE. First, we observed associations of multiple forms of trauma exposure to DE outcomes in childhood and adulthood. Second, we found evidence for longitudinal associations of trauma exposure with DE among children but limited evidence for this relation among adults. Conversely, PTSD symptoms had significant associations with subsequent DE among adults, but we did not observe this relation in childhood.

The association of DE (particularly binge-purge symptoms) with exposure to both violent and sexual trauma has been documented among children, adolescents, and adults (e.g., Dansky et al., 1997; Smolak & Murnen, 2002). Consistent with this, we saw significant associations of violent trauma with each DE symptom cluster assessed in childhood and adulthood. Sexual trauma was linked with all outcomes assessed in childhood but with only BN symptoms, sustained appetite changes, and preoccupation with eating in adulthood. This may further suggest specific associations of sexual trauma with BN symptoms (i.e., versus AN symptoms) but could also reflect lower frequencies of lifetime sexual trauma and AN symptoms in this sample.

We did not anticipate the association of non-violent, non-sexual trauma in childhood with multiple forms of DE in that developmental period or the relation of cumulative lifetime exposure to such trauma with some forms of DE in adulthood. We note that non-violent, non-sexual trauma as defined here included instances of observing death or injury to others. It thus may have inadvertently captured the impact of witnessing violence (e.g., family violence).

Contrary to hypothesis, childhood exposure to non-sexual, non-violent trauma was related to some forms of DE in adulthood, whereas we observed no significant relations between violent or sexual trauma in childhood and adulthood DE. These results contrast slightly with those of Johnson et al. (2002), which found associations of childhood sexual abuse and physical neglect with both DE and diagnosable eating disorders in adulthood. Differences in follow-up period (i.e., through age 30 here versus age 22 in the earlier work) may have contributed to the discrepancy. We also controlled for childhood DE symptoms in our analyses; the impact of childhood trauma exposures on DE in adulthood may be mediated by childhood DE. Further research should continue to target high-risk groups to prospectively assess the relation of maltreatment and other childhood trauma exposures on adulthood DE.

Within developmental periods, trauma exposures but not PTSD symptoms had significant associations with DE in childhood. The reverse was true in adulthood. This suggests possible differential pathways from trauma exposure to DE by developmental time period. Among youth, mood and anxiety symptoms may be even more common following trauma exposure than PTSD symptoms (Copeland et al., 2007). Future research should test whether these mediate the relation between trauma exposure and DE in childhood and adolescence. PTSD symptoms may represent a more important target among adults. Although we cannot rule out that the longer timeframe between assessments in adulthood impacted our findings, our results echo previous work showing that BN was more prevalent among adult women sexual assault survivors with a lifetime history of PTSD versus those who did not experience PTSD (Dansky et al., 1997).

Trim, Galovski, Wagner, & Brewerton (2017) suggested potential functions of DE symptoms among individuals with PTSD, including downregulating hyperarousal or responding to negative cognitions about shape and weight stemming from trauma experiences. We found significant relations for painful recall (which encompasses distress associated with this reexperiencing) and trending relations for hyperarousal, suggesting that BN symptoms may function to counteract intrusive traumatic memories and to downregulate arousal. If confirmed, these initial results support the importance of examining specific PTSD symptom clusters for differential effects on DE.

A key strength of this study is its use of a diverse, community-based sample that participated in repeated assessments over a 16-year follow-up period. Trained interviewers gathered the data, and childhood data collection included parent report, likely mitigating some of the bias inherent in self-report. We were also able to clarify the relation of trauma exposure versus PTSD symptoms on DE and examine the relations of specific PTSD symptom clusters with DE in adulthood.

The community-based sample also reflects a limitation, however, in that prevalence of DE symptoms was relatively low. Such low prevalence (and resulting reduction in power) is consistent with the relatively low base rate of DE symptoms in the population as a whole and reflects the challenge of completing population-based, longitudinal research on DE. Although trauma exposure was unfortunately widespread in the sample, PTSD symptoms were less common, particularly during childhood. It is possible that the prevalence of PTSD symptoms in childhood was underestimated due to the screening process for such symptoms. Additionally, both PTSD and DE symptoms were assessed using DSM-IV criteria rather than DSM-5, and neither the CAPA or YAPA disordered eating modules were independently validated. Replication of the findings using established DE and PTSD measures for DSM-5 and in clinical samples are critical next steps. Another important limitation was that time between assessments and screening criteria for the full PTSD module differed from childhood to adulthood observations. We thus cannot directly compare the findings across developmental periods.

Despite these limitations, the study provides new longitudinal evidence for associations of trauma exposure and PTSD symptoms with later DE. The findings also point to the impact that PTSD symptoms have on symptoms of BN among adults. Continued efforts to understand the cognitive, affective, and interpersonal mechanisms connecting trauma exposure to specific DE symptoms among children and adults will be critical to developing prevention and clinical intervention techniques that are both developmentally sensitive and effective.

Acknowledgments

We gratefully acknowledge the efforts of all GSMS staff, along with the participants and their parents.

Disclosures

None of the author(s) have any conflicts of interest to disclose.

Funding

This work was supported by the National Institute of Mental Health (MH117559,MH63970, MH63671, MH48085, and MH080230), National Institute of Drug Abuse (DA/MH11301), and the Eunice Kennedy Shriver National Institute of Child Health and Human Development (HD093651). The views expressed in this manuscript represent those of the authors and not those of the U.S. Government or Department of Veterans Affairs;National Institute on Drug Abuse [DA/MH11301];

ORCID

Rachel L. Zelkowitz http://orcid.org/0000-0002-3083-4669
Nancy L. Zucker http://orcid.org/0000-0003-2278-5008
William E. Copeland http://orcid.org/0000-0002-1348-7781

References

American Psychiatric Association. (2000). *Diagnostic and statistical manual of mental disorders* (4th ed.). Text Revision.

Angold, A., & Costello, E. J. (2000). The Child and Adolescent Psychiatric Assessment (CAPA). *Journal of the American Academy of Child and Adolescent Psychiatry*, *39*(1), 39–48. https://doi.org/10.1097/00004583-200001000-00015

Angold, A., Prendergast, M., Cox, A., Harrington, R., Simonoff, E., & Rutter, M. (1995). The Child and Adolescent Psychiatric Assessment (CAPA). *Psychological Medicine*, *25*(4), 739–753. https://doi.org/10.1017/S003329170003498X

Brewerton, T. D. (2007). Eating disorders, trauma, and comorbidity: Focus on PTSD. *Eating Disorders*, *15*(4), 285–304. https://doi.org/10.1080/10640260701454311

Caslini, M., Bartoli, F., Crocamo, C., Dakanalis, A., Clerici, M., & Carrà, G. (2016). Disentangling the association between child abuse and eating disorders: A systematic review and meta-analysis. *Psychosomatic Medicine*, *78*(1), 79–90. https://doi.org/10.1097/PSY.0000000000000233

Copeland, W. E., Bulik, C. M., Zucker, N., Wolke, D., Lereya, S. T., & Costello, E. J. (2015). Does childhood bullying predict eating disorder symptoms? A prospective, longitudinal analysis: Eating disorders and bullying. *International Journal of Eating Disorders*, *48*(8), 1141–1149. https://doi.org/10.1002/eat.22459

Copeland, W. E., Keeler, G., Angold, A., & Costello, E. J. (2007). Traumatic events and posttraumatic stress in childhood. *Archives of General Psychiatry*, *64*(5), 577. https://doi.org/10.1001/archpsyc.64.5.577

Copeland, W. E., Shanahan, L., Hinesley, J., Chan, R. F., Aberg, K. A., Fairbank, J. A., Van Den Oord, E. J. C. G., & Costello, E. J. (2018). Association of childhood trauma exposure with adult psychiatric disorders and functional outcomes. *JAMA Network Open*, *1*(7), e184493. https://doi.org/10.1001/jamanetworkopen.2018.4493

Copeland, W. E., Wolke, D., Shanahan, L., & Costello, E. J. (2015). Adult Functional Outcomes of Common Childhood Psychiatric Problems: A Prospective, Longitudinal Study. *JAMA Psychiatry*, *72*(9), 892. https://doi.org/10.1001/jamapsychiatry.2015.0730

Costello, E. J. (1996). The great smoky mountains study of youth: Goals, design, methods, and the prevalence of DSM-III-R disorders. *Archives of General Psychiatry*, *53*(12), 1129. https://doi.org/10.1001/archpsyc.1996.01830120067012

Costello, E. J., Copeland, W., & Angold, A. (2016). The great smoky mountains study: Developmental epidemiology in the southeastern United States. *Social Psychiatry and Psychiatric Epidemiology*, *51*(5), 639–646. https://doi.org/10.1007/s00127-015-1168-1

Cronce, J. M., Bedard-Gilligan, M. A., Zimmerman, L., Hodge, K. A., & Kaysen, D. (2017). Alcohol and binge eating as mediators between posttraumatic stress disorder symptom severity and body mass index: Alcohol and Binge Eating Between PTSD and BMI. *Obesity*, *25*(4), 801–806. https://doi.org/10.1002/oby.21809

Dansky, B. S., Brewerton, T. D., Kilpatrick, D. G., & O'Neil, P. M. (1997). The National Women's study: Relationship of victimization and posttraumatic stress disorder to bulimia nervosa. *The International Journal of Eating Disorders*, *21*(3), 213–228. https://doi.org/10.1002/(SICI)1098-108X(199704)21:3<213::AID-EAT2>3.0.CO;2-N

Dubosc, A., Capitaine, M., Franko, D. L., Bui, E., Brunet, A., Chabrol, H., & Rodgers, R., . F. (2012). Early adult sexual assault and disordered eating: The mediating role of posttraumatic stress symptoms. *Journal of Traumatic Stress*, *25*(1), 50–56. https://doi.org/10.1002/jts.21664

Holzer, S. R., Uppala, S., Wonderlich, S. A., Crosby, R. D., & Simonich, H. (2008). Mediational significance of PTSD in the relationship of sexual trauma and eating disorders. *Child Abuse & Neglect*, *32*(5), 561–566. https://doi.org/10.1016/j.chiabu.2007.07.011

Huston, J. C., Grillo, A. R., Iverson, K. M., & Mitchell, K. S. (2019). Associations between disordered eating and intimate partner violence mediated by depression and posttraumatic stress disorder symptoms in a female veteran sample. *General Hospital Psychiatry*, *58*, 77–82. https://doi.org/10.1016/j.genhosppsych.2019.03.007

Jacobson, I. G., Smith, T. C., Smith, B., Keel, P. K., Amoroso, P. J., Wells, T. S., Bathalon, G. P., Boyko, E. J., & Ryan, M. A. K., & for the Millennium Cohort Study Team. (2008). Disordered eating and weight changes after deployment: Longitudinal assessment of a large US military cohort. *American Journal of Epidemiology*, *169*(4), 415–427. doi: 10.1093/aje/kwn366

Johnson, J. G., Cohen, P., Kasen, S., & Brook, J. S. (2002). Childhood adversities associated with risk for eating disorders or weight problems during adolescence or early adulthood. *American Journal of Psychiatry*, *159*(3), 394–400. https://doi.org/10.1176/appi.ajp.159.3.394

Lipson, S. K., & Sonneville, K. R. (2020). Understanding suicide risk and eating disorders in college student populations: Results from a national study. *International Journal of Eating Disorders*, *53*(2), 229–238. https://doi.org/10.1002/eat.23188

Mason, S. M., Frazier, P. A., Austin, S. B., Harlow, B. L., Jackson, B., Raymond, N. C., & Rich-Edwards, J. W. (2017). Posttraumatic stress disorder symptoms and problematic overeating behaviors in young men and women. *Annals of Behavioral Medicine*, *51*(6), 822–832. https://doi.org/10.1007/s12160-017-9905-1

Mitchell, K. S., Mazzeo, S. E., Schlesinger, M. R., Brewerton, T. D., & Smith, B. N. (2012). Comorbidity of partial and subthreshold PTSD among men and women with eating disorders in the national comorbidity survey-replication study. *The International Journal of Eating Disorders*, *45*(3), 307–315. https://doi.org/10.1002/eat.20965

Mitchell, K. S., Porter, B., Boyko, E. J., & Field, A. E. (2016). Longitudinal associations among posttraumatic stress disorder, disordered eating, and weight gain in military men and women. *American Journal of Epidemiology*, *184*(1), 33–47. https://doi.org/10.1093/aje/kwv291

Molendijk, M. L., Hoek, H. W., Brewerton, T. D., & Elzinga, B. M. (2017). Childhood maltreatment and eating disorder pathology: A systematic review and dose-response meta-analysis. *Psychological Medicine*, *47*(8), 1402–1416. https://doi.org/10.1017/S0033291716003561

Neumark-Sztainer, D., Wall, M., Larson, N. I., Eisenberg, M. E., & Loth, K. (2011). Dieting and disordered eating behaviors from adolescence to young adulthood: Findings from a 10-Year longitudinal study. *Journal of the American Dietetic Association, 111*(7), 1004–1011. https://doi.org/10.1016/j.jada.2011.04.012

Pignatelli, A. M., Wampers, M., Loriedo, C., Biondi, M., & Vanderlinden, J. (2017). Childhood neglect in eating disorders: A systematic review and meta-analysis. *Journal of Trauma & Dissociation: The Official Journal of the International Society for the Study of Dissociation (ISSD), 18*(1), 100–115. https://doi.org/10.1080/15299732.2016.1198951

Sanci, L., Coffey, C., Olsson, C., Reid, S., Carlin, J. B., & Patton, G. (2008). Childhood sexual abuse and eating disorders in females: Findings from the Victorian adolescent health cohort study. *Archives of Pediatrics & Adolescent Medicine, 162*(3), 261–267. https://doi.org/10.1001/archpediatrics.2007.58

Smolak, L., & Murnen, S. K. (2002). A meta-analytic examination of the relationship between child sexual abuse and eating disorders. *The International Journal of Eating Disorders, 31*(2), 136–150. https://doi.org/10.1002/eat.10008

Solmi, F., Sonneville, K. R., Easter, A., Horton, N. J., Crosby, R. D., Treasure, J., Rodriguez, A., Jarvelin, M. R., Field, A. E., & Micali, N. (2015). Prevalence of purging at age 16 and associations with negative outcomes among girls in three community-based cohorts. *Journal of Child Psychology and Psychiatry, 56*(1), 87–96. https://doi.org/10.1111/jcpp.12283

Stice, E., & Bearman, S. K. (2001). Body-image and eating disturbances prospectively predict increases in depressive symptoms in adolescent girls: A growth curve analysis. *Developmental Psychology, 37*(5), 597–607. https://doi.org/10.1037/0012-1649.37.5.597

Swanson, S. A., Crow, S. J., Le Grange, D., Swendsen, J., & Merikangas, K. R. (2011). Prevalence and Correlates of Eating Disorders in Adolescents: Results From the National Comorbidity Survey Replication Adolescent Supplement. *Archives of General Psychiatry, 68*(7), 714. https://doi.org/org/10.1001/archgenpsychiatry.2011.22

Trim, J. G., Galovski, T. E., Wagner, A., & Brewerton, T. D. (2017). Treating eating disorder–posttraumatic stress disorder patients: A synthesis of the literature and new treatment directions. L. K. Anderson, S. B. Murray, & W. H. Kaye, Eds., *Clinical handbook of complex and atypical eating disorders.* 40–59 By J. G. Trim, T. E. Galovski, A. Wagner, & T. D. Brewerton. Oxford University Press. https://doi.org/10.1093/med-psych/9780190630409.003.0003.

Trottier, K., & MacDonald, D. E. (2017). Update on psychological trauma, other severe adverse experiences and eating disorders: State of the research and future research directions. *Current Psychiatry Reports, 19*(8), 45. https://doi.org/10.1007/s11920-017-0806-6

Trottier, K., Wonderlich, S. A., Monson, C. M., Crosby, R. D., & Olmsted, M. P. (2016). Investigating posttraumatic stress disorder as a psychological maintaining factor of eating disorders: Eating disorders and posttraumatic stress disorder. *International Journal of Eating Disorders, 49*(5), 455–457. https://doi.org/10.1002/eat.22516

Vanzhula, I. A., Calebs, B., Fewell, L., & Levinson, C. A. (2019). Illness pathways between eating disorder and post-traumatic stress disorder symptoms: Understanding comorbidity with network analysis. *European Eating Disorders Review, 27*(2), 147–160. https://doi.org/10.1002/erv.2634

Genetic and environmental influences on posttraumatic stress disorder symptoms and disinhibited eating behaviors

Niloofar Afari, Marianna Gasperi, Cara Dochat, Jennalee S. Wooldridge, Matthew S. Herbert, Ellen A. Schur, and Dedra S. Buchwald

ABSTRACT

Posttraumatic stress disorder (PTSD) and eating disorders (ED) frequently co-occur, but the mechanisms underlying this association remain unclear. EDs are characterized by features of maladaptive eating behaviors including disinhibited eating and cognitive dietary restraint. Identifying the genetic overlap between PTSD symptoms and maladaptive eating behaviors may elucidate biological mechanisms and potential treatment targets. A community sample of 400 same-sex twins (102 monozygotic and 98 dizygotic pairs) completed the PTSD Checklist-Civilian (PCL-C) for PTSD symptoms and the Three-Factor Eating Questionnaire-Reduced (TFEQ-R18) for eating behaviors (uncontrolled eating, emotional eating, and cognitive dietary restraint). We used biometric modeling to examine the genetic and environmental relationships between PCL-C and TFEQ-R18 total and subscales scores. Heritability was estimated at 48% for PTSD symptoms and 45% for eating behavior overall. Bivariate models revealed a significant genetic correlation between PTSD symptoms and eating behavior overall (r_q =.34; CI:.07,.58) and Uncontrolled Eating (r_g =.53; CI:.24,.84), and a significant environmental correlation between PTSD symptoms and Emotional Eating (r_e =.30; CI:.12,.45). These findings suggest the influence of common etiology. Future research and clinical efforts should focus on developing integrated treatments.

Clinical implicationsThere is genetic overlap between PTSD symptoms and uncontrolled eating behavior.There is non-shared environmental overlap between PTSD symptoms and emotional eating.Further investigation into underlying biological mechanisms shared by PTSD and eating disorder symptoms is warranted.Identifying common environmental risk and protective factors shared by PTSD and eating disorder symptoms may facilitate treatment.

Clinical implications

- There is genetic overlap between PTSD symptoms and uncontrolled eating behavior.
- There is non-shared environmental overlap between PTSD symptoms and emotional eating.
- Further investigation into underlying biological mechanisms shared by PTSD and eating disorder symptoms is warranted.
- Identifying common environmental risk and protective factors shared by PTSD and eating disorder symptoms may facilitate treatment.

Posttraumatic stress disorder (PTSD) is a psychological condition that may develop following exposure to trauma and is characterized by unwanted thoughts and feelings related to the event, distress in response to trauma-related cues, emotional numbness and avoidance, and increased arousal. PTSD is highly comorbid with eating disorders (ED) including Bulimia Nervosa (BN), Binge Eating Disorder (BED), and Anorexia Nervosa (AN) binge-eating/purging type, and trauma exposure has been suggested as a risk factor for the development of ED (Brewerton, 2007; K. S. Mitchell et al., 2012). Over 40% of individuals with PTSD surveyed in a large population-based study reported maladaptive eating symptoms (Sommer et al., 2018), where respondents with subthreshold or threshold PTSD reported significantly greater binge eating symptoms than did respondents with a trauma history but no PTSD or low PTSD symptoms (Braun et al., 2019). Patients with co-occurring PTSD and ED show a higher prevalence of psychiatric and substance use comorbidities and more severe ED symptoms than their counterparts with either condition alone (Grilo et al., 2012; Scharff et al., 2019).

Despite substantial research on the prevalence and negative sequelae of co-occurring PTSD and ED, little is known about shared mechanisms and causal relationships. Shared mechanisms may be genetic, neurobiological, and psychological in nature. PTSD and ED symptoms may be functionally related, such that ED symptoms (e.g., binge eating and emotional eating behaviors, etc.) serve as an effort to downregulate PTSD-consistent hyperarousal or serve trauma-related escape and avoidance functions (Breland et al., 2018; Trottier et al., 2016). Elucidating the mechanisms underlying the comorbidity of PTSD and ED symptoms may provide support for developing integrated treatments (Trottier & MacDonald, 2017).

Most research exploring the comorbidity of PTSD and ED has examined individual eating disorders; however, latent class analyses, genetics research, and epidemiological findings support examining maladaptive eating behaviors that are common to several EDs and may also be common phenotypic features of PTSD (K. Mitchell et al., 2010; Sommer et al., 2018; Von Lojewski et al., 2012). These maladaptive eating behaviors include but are not limited to (1) disinhibited eating behavior, and (2) cognitive dietary restraint, characterized by a set of self-imposed rules to control food intake for weight loss or to control body weight. The construct of disinhibited eating subsumes related but distinct eating behaviors, some of which are characterized by loss of control and objectively large intake (i.e., sub-diagnostic threshold binge eating) and others which are characterized by a perceived lack of control and may or may not include objectively large intake but are distressing to the individual (e.g., uncontrolled eating, emotional eating) (Johnson et al., 2012; Vainik et al., 2015). Though past research has demonstrated that these eating behaviors are associated *with* and are potential risk factors *for* disordered eating (Anderson et al., 2016; Schaumberg & Anderson, 2016), only a handful of studies have examined the association between PTSD symptoms and disinhibited eating (S. M. Mason et al., 2017; Talbot et al., 2013). For example, previous research on the relationship between PTSD and AN has demonstrated the restricting subtype of AN is less strongly associated with PTSD than the AN binge eating/purging type (e.g., Brewerton, 2007; Carter et al, 2006; Reyes-Rodríguez, 2011), suggesting that binge eating and other disinhibited eating features of EDs may be important for understanding the link between EDs and PTSD. Additionally, the only study evaluating the association of PTSD symptoms with cognitive dietary restraint failed to find a significant relationship (J. E. Mason et al., 2019). Improving our understanding of the relationship between PTSD symptoms and transdiagnostic maladaptive eating behaviors may help elucidate the mechanisms underlying the spectrum of ED and their association with PTSD.

Twin studies, which compare monozygotic (MZ) and dizygotic (DZ) twins using biometric modeling, provide a unique opportunity to test the importance of neurobiological and psychosocial mechanisms by estimating both genetic and environmental influences on complex phenotypes. Twin studies can explain the degree to which phenotypic associations between two or more traits are due to shared genetic or environmental factors. Understanding the extent to which various etiological factors (e.g., genetic or environmental) contribute to the co-occurrence of phenotypes has important implications. For instance, if the same genes are found to contribute to both phenotypes, this lends support for a common biological predisposition or pathway and would have substantial implications for identifying specific common genes. Conversely, if the association among phenotypes is due primarily to environmental reasons, prevention and intervention efforts should focus on appropriate strategies to address environmental factors such as psychosocial adversity or trauma. These scenarios represent two theoretical extremes with a more likely scenario involving both genetic and environmental influences.

Previous twin research has demonstrated moderate levels of heritability for PTSD (Kremen et al., 2012), ED, and maladaptive eating behaviors (Thornton et al., 2010). Heritability estimates for PTSD and PTSD symptoms range from 30% to 72%, depending on the population (Kremen et al., 2012; Sartor et al.,

2011). Estimates for the heritability of disinhibited eating alone range from 18% to 45%; findings for cognitive dietary restraint have been mixed due to varying definitions and measures, but estimated genetic influences of up to 59% have been reported (Thornton et al., 2011). Despite the known heritability of these phenotypes individually, no studies have evaluated the contribution of genetic and environmental influences to the co-occurrence of PTSD symptoms and disinhibited and other maladaptive eating behaviors. Thus, the aim of our study was to evaluate potential genetic and environmental sources of co-occurrence between PTSD symptoms and disinhibited eating (i.e., uncontrolled eating and emotional eating) and cognitive dietary restraint in a genetically informatic sample of non-clinical, community-dwelling twins. Based on previous research, we expected that all traits would be genetically influenced, and hypothesized that the covariation between PTSD symptoms and disinhibited eating behaviors would be due, in part, to common genetic factors. Given the very limited prior research, we had no hypotheses regarding PTSD and cognitive dietary restraint.

Methods

Participants

Participants were same-sex twins from the Washington State Twin Registry (WSTR; previously known as the University of Washington Twin Registry), a community-based sample drawn from information gathered by the Washington State Department of Licensing (Strachan et al., 2013). This randomly selected subset was originally recruited for a study examining the psychosocial, demographic, and clinical factors associated with experimental pain sensitivity. A detailed description of Registry participant recruitment procedures are described elsewhere (Afari et al., 2006; Strachan et al., 2013). Same-sex twin pairs between 18 and 65 years of age were eligible. Of the 752 individuals who were screened for participation, 75 individuals (one or both of a twin pair) did not meet the inclusion criteria. These participants were excluded for use of opioid or other prescription pain medications, immune-modulating medications, a BMI of <18.5 kg/m^2, current or anticipated pregnancy, a neuropathy, and ongoing cancer treatment, as these could interfere with the parent experimental pain study measurements. In addition, 77 eligible pairs were unable to participate due to scheduling issues. The final sample consisted of 400 non-clinical members of the WSTR consisting of 102 monozygotic (MZ) and 98 dizygotic (DZ) same-sex twin pairs. The twins (63% female) were mostly young to middle-aged adults (M = 29 years, SD = 12, range = 19–65), and most were White (80%).

Zygosity was determined using either the AmpFlSTR Identifiler Plus PCR Amplification Kit or the PowerPlex 16 HS System. The two protocols are nearly identical, and all assays were conducted per manufacturer's instructions at the University of Washington Center for Clinical Genomics. Study procedures and protocols were approved by the Institutional Review Board at the University of Washington, and informed consent was obtained from participants.

Measures

PTSD symptoms

The PTSD Checklist-Civilian Version (PCL-C) (Weathers et al., 1993) is a self-report questionnaire consisting of 17 items that correspond to Diagnostic and Statistical Manual of Mental Disorders, Fourth Edition (DSM-IV) (American Psychiatric Association, 2000) diagnostic criteria for PTSD. Participants report the extent to which 17 symptoms (e.g., "repeated, disturbing memories, thoughts, or images of a stressful experience from the past") have caused distress in the past four weeks using a 5-point scale from 1 (*not at all*) to 5 (*extremely*). Because identifying a PTSD Criterion A trauma exposure is not required on the PCL-C, this measure assesses PTSD symptom burden in the context of stressful life events rather than a specific previous trauma. Item responses are summed to calculate a total score, which ranges from 17 to 85. Higher scores indicate a greater burden of PTSD symptoms. Different cutoff scores are used to examine the estimated prevalence of PTSD in different populations or settings, with a cutoff of 30–35 suggested for general population samples (National Center for PTSD, n.d.). The PCL-C has high internal consistency and strong agreement with the Clinician Administered PTSD Scale (Yeager et al., 2007) as well as the Composite International Diagnostic Interview PTSD module, $r = 0.90$ (Magruder et al., 2015). The mean PCL-C score was 29.7 (SD = 12.5) in a civilian primary care sample (Stein, McQquaid, Pedrelli, Lenox, & McCahill, 2000).

Eating behavior

The Three-Factor Eating Questionnaire Reduced (TFEQ-R18) (Karlsson et al., 2000) is an 18-item self-report questionnaire used to assess cognitive dietary restraint (conscious restriction of food intake with the intent to control body weight and/or to promote weight loss), uncontrolled eating (the tendency to eat more than usual due to a loss of control over intake accompanied by a subjective feeling of hunger), and emotional eating (inability to resist emotional cues, eating as a response to different negative emotions). The TFEQ-R18 is a revised and reduced version of the original 51-item TFEQ (Stunkard & Messick, 1985), also called the Eating Inventory, a commonly used measure of eating behaviors. Sample items include: "I consciously hold back at meals in order not to gain weight" (Cognitive Restraint); "Sometimes when I start eating, I just can't seem to stop" (Uncontrolled Eating); and "When I feel lonely, I console myself by eating" (Emotional Eating). Participants rate the extent to which each statement is true on a 4-point scale from 4 (*definitely true*) to 1 (*definitely false*) for the first 17 questions. The final question asks participants to rate the extent of their restrained eating from 1 (*no restraint in eating*) to 8 (*total restraint*). All items are summed into a total score, and subsets are summed to create three subscale scores. Higher scores indicate greater symptoms (De Lauzon et al., 2004). Previous studies have reported strong internal consistency and reliability of the TFEQ-R18 total and subscale scores (Karlsson et al., 2000). To our knowledge, there are no norms for the TFEQ-R18 and no suggested cutoff scores. Mean subscale scores in a study of the psychometric properties of the Spanish version of the measure in a non-clinical sample were: Uncontrolled Eating (17.50 ± 6.20); Cognitive Restraint (11.69 ± 4.11); and Emotional Eating (5.14 ± 2.65) (Jáuregui-Lobera, García-Cruz, Carbonero-Carreño, Magallares, & Ruiz-Prieto, 2014).

Statistical analyses

Descriptive statistics were calculated using means and standard deviations, and study variables were compared by sex. For the remainder of the analyses, individual variables were age and sex-regressed following standard analytic procedures (McGue & Bouchard, 1984) and log-transformed to better approximate normality. Standard biometric models were used to evaluate the relative contribution of genetic and environmental factors to each phenotype. The classical twin model estimates variance components based on similarities among MZ twins who share 100% and DZ twins who share, on average, 50% of their segregating genes. Using univariate biometric models, phenotypic variance is decomposed into genetic and environm ental sources of variance, including additive genetic influence (A), shared environmental influences (C), and non-shared environmental influences (E). Shared environmental influences are influences that make members of a twin pair more similar to one another, while non-shared environmental influences are specific to the individual and also capture measurement error. Three subsequent submodels were computed that dropped shared environmental influences (AE model), genetic influences (CE model), and genetic and shared environmental influences (E model). The univariate models were extended to a bivariate Cholesky decomposition (Neale & Maes, 2004) to determine the degree of genetic and environmental overlap between two variables, such as PTSD symptoms and Emotional Eating (Figure 1a). Latent factors A_1, C_1, and E_1 account for the additive genetic and shared environmental variance in the first phenotype, including the variance that overlaps with risk for the second. Residual additive genetic and non-shared environmental factors (independent of the first phenotype) are captured by Factors A_2, C_2, and E_2. Diagonal paths (a_{21}, c_{21}, e_{21})

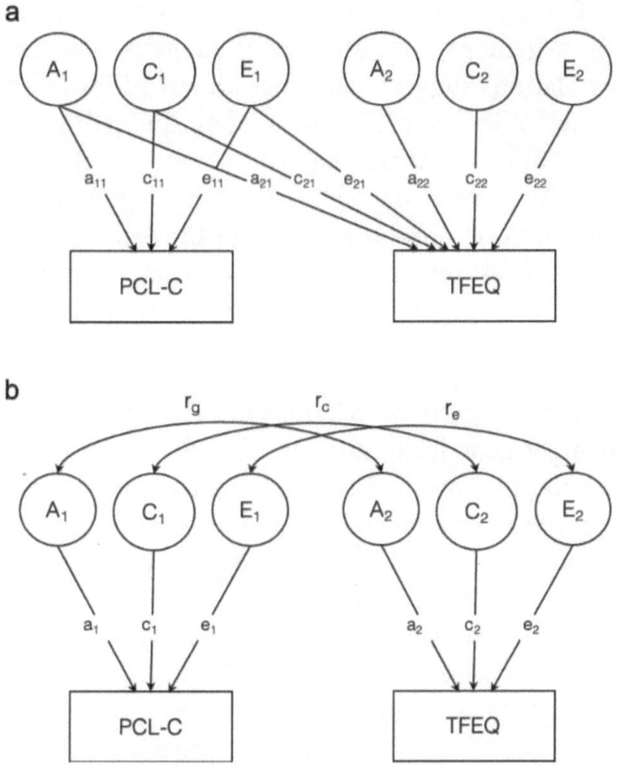

Figure 1. Path diagram of the bivariate Cholesky decomposition (a) of PCL-C and TFEQ-R18 eating variables and the correlated factors model (b). For simplicity, only one twin of a pair is shown. Variance of each phenotype (in squares) is decomposed into A = additive genetic influences, C = shared environmental influences, E = non-shared environmental influences (in circles). Within the Cholesky decomposition (a), paths a_{11}, c_{11}, and e_{11} are influences on PCL-C, diagonal paths a_{21}, c_{21}, e_{21} are influences on the covariance between PCL-C and TFEQ-R18 eating variables, and paths a_{22}, c_{22}, e_{22} are influences unique to eating variables. Parameter estimates from the Cholesky decomposition are used to construct other quantities of interest depicted in the correlated factors model (b), including the genetic correlation (r_g) and environmental correlations (r_c, r_e).

represent the genetic or environmental covariance between traits. The parameter estimates generated by the Cholesky decomposition were used to construct other quantities of interest represented by the correlated factors model (Figure 1b)(Loehlin, 1996). Standardizing the genetic covariance on the genetic variance of the two phenotypes from the bivariate Cholesky decomposition yielded the genetic correlation, $r_g = \frac{a_{11}a_{21}}{\sqrt{a_{11}^2\left(a_{21}^2+a_{22}^2\right)}}$, which indexed the magnitude of the genetic overlap between the two phenotypes, or the extent to which the same genes or environmental factors contribute to the observed phenotypic correlation between two variables (Loehlin, 1996). By estimating the overlap in genetic signal rather than all sources of variance and covariance, genetic correlations are more informative than phenotypic correlations by isolating the source of the association (Neale & Maes, 2004). A genetic correlation of 1.0 suggests that the two variables share of all their genetic influences, while a genetic correlation of 0 suggests genetic independence. High genetic correlations suggest that genes identified for one trait would also likely influence the other trait. Similar analytic procedures can be used to estimate shared (r_c) and non-shared environmental correlations (r_e). Squaring the genetic correlation provides an estimate of the degree to which the genetic factors associated with one variable account for the genetic risk associated with other. Using the path estimates from the Cholesky decomposition, we also estimated the degree of genetic contribution to the phenotypic correlation between two variables, $prop_A = \frac{r_A\sqrt{a_{11}^2\left(a_{21}^2+a_{22}^2\right)}}{r}$. This approach is particularly valuable when the phenotypic correlations are low, but the observed association may be strongly genetically influenced. Contribution of environmental factors to the phenotypic correlation were calculated in an analogous manner.

Models were fit to the raw data using full information maximum-likelihood in OpenMx software version 2.12.1 (M. C. Neale et al., 2016) in the software R (R Core Team, 2016). This approach allows the use of all available information from all cases regardless of missing data and yields less-biased estimates when compared to listwise or pairwise deletion methods (Allison, 2003). Adequacy of model fit was evaluated using −2 times the natural log-likelihood (−2lnL) and Akaike's Information Criterion (AIC) between nested models. Lower AIC values signify a better balance between goodness of fit and parsimony. The goal is to identify the most parsimonious model that sufficiently describes the data, and models with fewer parameters are preferred if they do not result in a significant deterioration of fit. Significance of parameters was tested using the ($\chi 2$) difference test, comparing the goodness-of-fit of the reduced model to a fuller model.

Results

The means and standard deviations for all study measures for the entire sample and by sex are presented in (Table 1). Only 20 individual item responses were missing (<1%) from both questionnaires. Little's missing

Table 1. Means and standard deviations for all study variables for the entire sample and by sex.

Measure*	Men (n = 188) Mean (SD)	Women (n = 212) Mean (SD)	Total (N = 400) Mean (SD)	p
PCL-C (17–67)	26.26 (9.39)	25.71 (8.85)	25.97 (9.10)	.545
TFEQ Total (18–63)	33.24 (7.67)	37.10 (8.24)	35.28 (8.20)	<.001
Cognitive Restraint (6–23)	11.38 (4.09)	13.62 (3.83)	12.57 (4.10)	<.001
Uncontrolled Eating (9–34)	17.34 (5.28)	17.80 (5.00)	17.58 (5.13)	.375
Emotional Eating (3–12)	4.52 (1.92)	5.68 (2.48)	5.13 (2.31)	<.001

Note. PCL-C = PTSD Checklist—Civilian Version; TFEQ = Three Factor Eating Questionnaire-Reduced 18; Cognitive Restraint = TFEQ-R18 Cognitive Restraint subscale; Uncontrolled Eating = TFEQ-R18 Uncontrolled Eating subscale; Emotional Eating = TFEQ-R18 Emotional Eating subscale.

* Range of obtained scores in parentheses.

completely at random (MCAR) test showed that any missing data were at random (Little's MCAR test: $\chi 2 = 446.377$, df = 440, $p = .407$). No participants were missing more than one item per scale, and scale scores were prorated for each respondent with missing data. The mean PCL-C and TFEQ-R18 subscale scores were similar to those previously reported in non-clinical samples (Jáuregui-Lobera et al., 2014; Stein et al., 2000). In our sample, 55 individuals (13.8%), with 25 men (13.3%) and 30 women (14.2%) met the National Center for PTSD (n.d.) suggested PCL-C cut-off of 35 for general population samples. This is similar to rates reported in the general population (National Center for PTSD, n.d.). The total TFEQ-R18 score and the Cognitive Restraint and Emotional Eating subscale scores for female twins were significantly higher than for male twins, supporting the decision to control for sex in the biometric and other analyses. The phenotypic correlations between PCL-C and TFEQ-R18 Total ($r = .32$, $p < .001$), Uncontrolled Eating ($r = .31$, $p < .001$), and Emotional Eating ($r = .29$, $p < .001$) were significant; the phenotypic correlation between PCL-C and Cognitive Restraint subscale score ($r = .08$, $p > .05$) was not significant. Because no phenotypic correlation between PCL-C and Cognitive Restraint was detected, genetic and non-shared environmental correlations were not calculated.

Biometric model fitting

Univariate biometric modeling evaluated the contribution of genetic and environmental influences on the variance in PCL-C and TFEQ-R18 total and subscales separately. The model fit results are presented in Supplemental (Table 1) and revealed that the AE models were the most parsimonious for all phenotypes, indicating no shared environmental influence on any of the variables. Bivariate Cholesky decompositions were used to estimate the degree of genetic and environmental overlap between PTSD and TFEQ-R18 scores.

Table 2. Standardized variance components from the AE bivariate models.

	Standardized Estimates (95% CI)	
Measure	a^2	e^2
PCL-C	.48 (.33;.61)	.52 (.39;.67)
TFEQ Total	.45 (.29;.58)	.55 (.42;.71)
Cognitive Restraint	.48 (.33;.60)	.52 (.40;.67)
Uncontrolled Eating	.34 (.17;.48)	.66 (.52;.83)
Emotional Eating	.34 (.16;.49)	.66 (.51;.84)

Note. PCL-C = PTSD Checklist—Civilian Version; TFEQ = Three Factor Eating Questionnaire-Reduced 18; Cognitive Restraint = TFEQ-R18 Cognitive Restraint subscale; Uncontrolled Eating = TFEQ-R18 Uncontrolled Eating subscale; Emotional Eating = TFEQ-R18 Emotional Eating subscale; CI = Confidence Interval; a^2 = additive genetic; e^2 = non-shared environment.

Table 3. Phenotypic, additive genetic correlations (r_g), and non-shared environmental correlations (r_e) between PCL-C and TFEQ, along with 95% confidence intervals from AE models.

		Proportion of Phenotypic Correlation			
Measure	Phenotypic Correlation with PCL-C total score (95% CI)	Genetic Effects	Environmental Effects	r_g (95% CI)	r_e (95% CI)
TFEQ Total	**.32 (.25;.40)**	51%	49%	**.34 (.07;.58)**	**.29 (.11;.45)**
Cognitive Restraint	.08 (.00;.21)	–*	–*	–*	–*
Uncontrolled Eating	**.31 (.23;.39)**	69%	31%	**.53 (.24;.84)**	.16 (−.01;.33)
Emotional Eating	**.29 (.22;.34)**	39%	61%	.27 (−.05;.57)	**.30 (.12;.45)**

Note: PCL-C = PTSD Checklist—Civilian Version; TFEQ = Three Factor Eating Questionnaire-Reduced 18; Cognitive Restraint = TFEQ-R18 Cognitive Restraint subscale; Uncontrolled Eating = TFEQ-R18 Uncontrolled Eating subscale; Emotional Eating = TFEQ-R18 Emotional Eating subscale; CI = Confidence Interval; r_g = genetic correlation; r_e = non-shared environmental correlation*

Not computed due to lack of phenotypic association. Significant correlations in bold.

Model fit results are presented in Supplemental (Table 2) and suggest that AE models, containing no shared environmental effects (path estimates from best fitting AE models in Supplemental Table 3), provided the best fit for all comparisons.

Heritability estimates from the bivariate models are presented in (Table 2). Heritability was estimated at .48 (95% CI: .33; .61) for PCL-C total score and .45 (95% CI: .29; .58) for TFEQ-R18 total score with the remaining variance due to non-shared environmental influences. Similarly, subscales of the TFEQ-R18 showed moderate heritability (a^2 = .48 to .34) with the remaining variance due to non-shared environmental influences.

Genetic and environmental correlations

Phenotypic, genetic, and environmental correlations between PCL-C total score and the TFEQ-R18 total and subscale scores are presented in (Table 3). The genetic correlation between PCL-C and TFEQ-R18 Total was r_g = .34 (95% CI: .07; .58) indicating that the genetic factors associated with PTSD symptoms accounted for 12% of the genetic risk associated with eating behavior in general (this statistic was obtained by squaring the genetic correlation: .34 × .34 = .12 × 100% = 12%). Of the subscales, only the association between PCL-C and Uncontrolled Eating showed significant genetic correlation, r_g = .53 (95% CI: .24; .84), suggesting that the genetic risk for PTSD symptoms accounted for 28% of the genetic risk in uncontrolled eating behaviors. Non-shared environmental correlations (r_e) were significant for PCL-C and TFEQ-R18 Total and Emotional Eating, suggesting moderate environmental overlap among these phenotypes. The non-significant genetic correlation between PCL-C and Emotional Eating, and the non-significant non-shared environmental correlation between PCL-C and Uncontrolled Eating trended towards significance, suggesting that being underpowered may have resulted in these effects being trend-level and that these should be investigated in future studies. Overall, 51% of the phenotypic association between PCL-C and TFEQ-R18 Total and 69% of the association between PCL-C and Uncontrolled Eating were due to genetic effects, while 61% of the association between PCL-C and Emotional Eating was due to non-shared environmental influences.

Discussion

This is the first study to examine the genetic and environmental relationships between PTSD symptoms and maladaptive eating behaviors, including different forms of disinhibited eating and cognitive dietary restraint. Consistent with previous research (Bulik et al., 2016; Sheerin et al., 2017), we found that PTSD symptoms and each of the eating behavior phenotypes were moderately heritable, even in this non-clinical sample of men and women. We found a robust phenotypic relationship between PTSD symptoms and eating behaviors in general, and specifically with uncontrolled eating and emotional eating behaviors but not with cognitive dietary restraint. Our findings also revealed genetic overlap between PTSD symptoms and maladaptive eating behavior in general and uncontrolled eating specifically.

Genetic correlations suggest that specific genetic variants that confer an increased risk for PTSD may also be involved in maladaptive eating behavior. The contribution of genetic influences to the phenotypic relationship between PTSD symptoms and uncontrolled eating as an instance of disinhibited eating is consistent with our hypothesis and extends the literature beyond phenotypic analyses to suggest common biological mechanisms may underlie the association between these two domains. Possible mechanisms include dysfunction in the brain reward circuit involved in emotion regulation, impulse control, and motivation, which has been implicated in PTSD (Fenster et al., 2018). Changes in reward circuitry and associated dopaminergic systems have also been associated with uncontrolled or binge eating, and a handful of small genetic studies have identified potential genetic variants (e.g., *DAT1* dopamine transporter gene, *DRD2* dopamine receptor gene) linked with reward sensitivity in binge eating (Kessler et al., 2016). Relatedly, research is emerging that trait disinhibition, the propensity to behave impulsively in several domains including eating behaviors, also explains recent engagement in risky/self-destructive behavior in people with high PTSD symptoms (Sadeh et al., 2018, 2015). As with other personality traits, genetic factors may contribute substantially to a disinhibited personality, and some studies have identified genes involved in dopaminergic and serotonergic neurotransmission in relation to trait disinhibition (Gray et al., 2018). Most recently, multivariate genomic structural equation modeling analyses have revealed several hundred unique variants associated with externalizing behavior (Linnér et al., 2020), laying the groundwork for further investigation into disinhibited behavior. Together with this prior research, our findings support the importance of continuing molecular genetics research to identify specific common genes related to these and other biological pathways that may facilitate the development of novel pharmacological therapeutics.

We found that our measure of cognitive dietary restraint was moderately heritable, but not phenotypically associated with PTSD symptoms. Previous heritability estimates for dietary restraint have varied, possibly due to variability in samples, and the use of various measures that capture slightly different constructs, with estimates ranging from 0% to 59% (B. M. Neale et al., 2003; Thornton et al., 2011). Some have argued that the Restraint Scale (Polivy et al., 1988) captures restrictive behaviors more often associated with pathological eating, whereas the restraint scale of the Dutch Eating Behavior Questionnaire (Van Strien et al., 1986) and cognitive restraint subscale of the original TFEQ (Stunkard & Messick, 1985) focus on restraint behaviors like dieting which are adaptive for weight loss-seeking populations (Schur et al., 2009). However, the TFEQ has undergone several iterations, and the cognitive dietary restraint subscale of the 18-item version no longer contains many of the original items that assessed dieting behavior, and previous efforts to establish heritability of the TFEQ (B. M. Neale et al., 2003) do not overlap with the TFEQ-R18. Our estimate of heritability for cognitive restraint, however, was similar to that reported in the only twin study that used the TFEQ-R18 (Keskitalo et al., 2008) which reported 26–63% heritability for cognitive restraint, 45–69% for uncontrolled eating, and 9–45% for emotional eating. Likewise, the only study examining TFEQ-R18 scores and PTSD symptoms (PCL-5) failed to detect an association with cognitive restraint but reported significant correlations with uncontrolled and emotional eating, suggesting that restraint and disinhibited eating may be differentially associated with PTSD (J. E. Mason et al., 2019). Whether this lack of association is due to the quality of measurement by the scale or a true lack of relationship remains unclear. Additional research is needed to refine the construct validity of cognitive restraint and to clarify its relationship to PTSD symptoms.

The findings of a non-shared environmental contribution to the relationship between PTSD symptoms and maladaptive eating behavior have implications for the assessment and treatment of these symptoms. These non-shared, or person-specific environmental influences contribute to differences among siblings (Plomin & Daniels, 2011). Identifying types of psychosocial adversity potentially contributing to both PTSD and maladaptive eating behavior may be important to improving our understanding of this relationship. Influences may include exposure to trauma, illnesses, and accidents. Likewise, protective environmental factors, such as access to and quality of mental health care socioeconomic factors, and social support, may lower the risk for both. Future research efforts may evaluate specific environmental influences associated with both domains.

Evidence for both genetic and environmental overlap between PTSD symptoms and maladaptive eating behavior supports the development of integrated treatments that use evidence-based approaches for co-occurring PTSD and ED conditions with prominent disinhibited eating behavior (Brewerton, 2019). Limited research suggests that concurrent cognitive behavior therapy for PTSD and ED may be effective (Trottier et al., 2017), and cognitive processing therapy improved both trauma and non-specific ED symptoms in a PTSD sample (i.e., impulse regulation, interoceptive awareness, interpersonal distrust, ineffectiveness, and maturity fears; K. S. Mitchell et al., 2012). Future research should evaluate the various treatment approaches with evidence for both PTSD and ED (e.g., cognitive behavioral therapy, dialectical behavioral therapy, exposure therapies), and determine whether concurrent or sequential treatment is most effective. Frontline ED clinicians report that it is important to address PTSD symptoms in ED treatment and that concurrently treating these conditions may be most beneficial despite concerns about negative side effects (e.g., worsening of PTSD symptoms when ED behavior is reduced). PTSD treatment programs may also be enhanced by incorporating routine screening for disinhibited eating, and if indicated, an evaluation of ED. While pharmacological therapeutics may be developed to impact the shared genetic and biological mechanisms, novel integrated behavioral interventions can also be designed to address the environmental mechanisms that may link these conditions.

This study has several limitations. First, our findings are based on data from a relatively small sample of twins. Although our methods were optimized by a nearly equal ratio of MZ to DZ twin pairs and continuous rather than binary measures of the phenotypes (binary measures decrease statistical power) (Verhulst, 2017), research with larger samples is necessary to replicate our findings. Second, we used standardized, validated self-report measures of PTSD symptoms and eating behaviors that are primarily meant to be used as screening measures. Use of structured diagnostic interview assessments including clinician-administered PTSD measures that require endorsement of trauma exposure would strengthen our conclusions and might extend these findings to diagnostic phenotypes of PTSD and ED. Our measure of eating behaviors (TFEQ-R18) does not have standard cut-offs, making it difficult to compare the prevalence of these eating behaviors in our sample to other populations. However, we were able to examine relationships between this measure and PCL-C in our sample, where the absolute scores and how they compare to other samples is not critical. Third, the use of a non-clinical set of twins with BMI over 18.5 potentially limits generalizability to clinical samples and highlights the need to extend this work to samples with more severe clinical pathology. Nonetheless, our community twin sample provides valuable information about the variability of these phenotypes in non-clinical populations. Fourth, we found and controlled for sex differences on some measures of maladaptive eating; however, we were unable to compare results across sex due to our sample size constraints. Examining the potential moderating effects of sex on heritability and the genetic and environmental correlations among PTSD, ED, and eating behaviors will illuminate the role of sex in the association between these phenotypes. Finally, because our data were cross-sectional, firm conclusions cannot be drawn about causation. Nonetheless, this study contributes to the current understanding of the potential mechanisms underlying the association between PTSD and selected maladaptive eating behaviors characteristic of ED.

In conclusion, we found genetic overlap between PTSD symptoms and uncontrolled eating. In contrast, we found environmental contributions to the association between PTSD symptoms and emotional eating, and no relationship between PTSD symptoms and cognitive dietary restraint. The genetic link between PTSD and uncontrolled eating highlights the need for additional biometric and molecular genetics research to further examine the shared risk factors and biological mechanisms responsible for the co-occurrence of PTSD, maladaptive eating, and ED symptoms. Additional studies should explore the interplay of genetic and environmental factors that protect against the development of PTSD symptoms, maladaptive eating behaviors, and ED. Research is also needed to further elucidate relationships between PTSD and cognitive dietary restraint. Our findings support development of integrated PTSD and ED treatments that target shared biological mechanisms and common phenotypic presentations.

Acknowledgments

The authors gratefully acknowledge the continued cooperation and participation of the members of the Washington State Twin Registry, without whom this research would not be possible.

Disclosure statement

None of the authors have any conflicts of interest to disclose.

Funding

This research was supported by the National Institutes of Health under grant RC2HL103416. Drs. Afari and Herbert and Ms. Dochat are partially supported by R01DK106415 from National Institute of Diabetes and Kidney Disease. Dr. Herbert is also supported by VA RR&D CDA Grant 1IK2RX002807-01A2. Dr. Wooldridge is supported by the VA Office of Academic Affiliation advanced fellowship in women's health. The views expressed in this paper are those of the authors and do not reflect the official policy or position of the funding agency, Department of Veterans Affairs, the United States Government, or any institutions with which the authors are affiliated.

ORCID

Niloofar Afari http://orcid.org/0000-0002-6489-378X
Marianna Gasperi http://orcid.org/0000-0003-4112-5232
Jennalee S. Wooldridge http://orcid.org/0000-0002-2815-5974
Matthew S. Herbert http://orcid.org/0000-0001-7395-6271

References

Afari, N., Noonan, C., Goldberg, J., Edwards, K., Gadepalli, K., Osterman, B., ... Buchwald, D. (2006). University of Washington Twin Registry: Construction and characteristics of a community-based twin registry. *Twin Research and Human Genetics*, *9*(6), 1023–1029. https://doi.org/10.1375/twin.9.6.1023

Allison, P. D. (2003). Missing data techniques for structural equation modeling. *Journal of Abnormal Psychology*, *112*(4), 545–557. https://doi.org/10.1037/0021-843X.112.4.545

American Psychiatric Association. (2000). *Diagnostic and statistical manual of mental disorders* (4th ed.).Author. [text rev].

Anderson, L. M., Reilly, E. E., Schaumberg, K., Dmochowski, S., & Anderson, D. A. (2016). Contributions of mindful eating, intuitive eating, and restraint to BMI, disordered eating, and meal consumption in college students. *Eating and Weight Disorders-Studies on Anorexia, Bulimia and Obesity*, *21*(1), 83–90. https://doi.org/10.1007/s40519-015-0210-3

Braun, J., El-Gabalawy, R., Sommer, J. L., Pietrzak, R. H., Mitchell, K., & Mota, N. (2019). Trauma exposure, DSM-5 posttraumatic stress, and binge eating symptoms: Results from a nationally representative sample. *The Journal of Clinical Psychiatry*, *80*(6), 19m12813. https://doi.org/10.4088/JCP.19m12813

Breland, J. Y., Donalson, R., Dinh, J. V., & Maguen, S. (2018). Trauma exposure and disordered eating: A qualitative study. *Women & Health*, *58*(2), 160–174. https://doi.org/10.1080/03630242.2017.1282398

Brewerton, T. D. (2007). Eating disorders, trauma, and comorbidity: Focus on PTSD. *Eating Disorders*, *15*(4), 285–304. https://doi.org/10.1080/10640260701454311

Brewerton, T. D. (2019). An overview of trauma-informed care and practice for eating disorders. *Journal of Aggression, Maltreatment & Trauma*, *28*(4), 445–462. https://doi.org/10.1080/10926771.2018.1532940

Bulik, C. M., Kleiman, S. C., & Yilmaz, Z. (2016). Genetic epidemiology of eating disorders. *Current Opinion in Psychiatry*, *29*(6), 383. https://doi.org/10.1097/YCO.0000000000000275

Carter, J. C., Bewell, C., Blackmore, E., & Woodside, D. B. (2006). The impact of childhood sexual abuse in anorexia nervosa. *Child Abuse & Neglect*, *30*(3), 257–269.

De Lauzon, B., Romon, M., Deschamps, V., Lafay, L., Borys, J.-M., Karlsson, J., ... Charles, M. A. (2004). the Fleurbaix Laventie Ville Sante (FLVS) study group: The Three-Factor Eating Questionnaire-R18 is able to distinguish among different eating patterns in a general population. *The Journal of Nutrition*, *134*(9), 2372–2380.

Fenster, R. J., Lebois, L. A., Ressler, K. J., & Suh, J. (2018). Brain circuit dysfunction in post-traumatic stress disorder: From mouse to man. *Nature Reviews. Neuroscience*, *19*(9), 535–551. https://doi.org/10.1038/s41583-018-0039-7

Gray, J. C., MacKillop, J., Weafer, J., Hernandez, K. M., Gao, J., Palmer, A. A., & de Wit, H. (2018). Genetic analysis of impulsive personality traits: Examination of a priori candidates and genome-wide variation. *Psychiatry Research*, *259*, 398–404. https://doi.org/10.1016/j.psychres.2017.10.047

Grilo, C. M., White, M. A., Barnes, R. D., & Masheb, R. M. (2012). Posttraumatic stress disorder in women with binge eating disorder in primary care. *Journal of Psychiatric Practice*, *18*(6), 408. https://doi.org/10.1097/01.pra.0000422738.49377.5e

Jáuregui-Lobera, I., García-Cruz, P., Carbonero-Carreño, R., Magallares, A., & Ruiz-Prieto, I. (2014). Psychometric properties of Spanish version of the Three-Factor Eating Questionnaire-R18 (Tfeq-Sp) and its relationship with some eating-and body image-related variables. *Nutrients*, *6*(12), 5619–5635.

Johnson, F., Pratt, M., & Wardle, J. (2012). Dietary restraint and self-regulation in eating behavior. *International Journal of Obesity*, *36*(5), 665–674. https://doi.org/10.1038/ijo.2011.156

Karlsson, J., Persson, L.-O., Sjöström, L., & Sullivan, M. (2000). Psychometric properties and factor structure of the Three-Factor Eating Questionnaire (TFEQ) in obese men and women. Results from the Swedish Obese Subjects (SOS) study. *International Journal of Obesity*, *24* (12), 1715–1725. https://doi.org/10.1038/sj.ijo.0801442

Keskitalo, K., Tuorila, H., Spector, T. D., Cherkas, L. F., Knaapila, A., Kaprio, J., ... Perola, M. (2008). The Three-Factor Eating Questionnaire, body mass index, and responses to sweet and salty fatty foods: A twin study of genetic and environmental associations. *The American Journal of Clinical Nutrition*, *88*(2), 263–271. https://doi.org/10.1093/ajcn/88.2.263

Kessler, R. M., Hutson, P. H., Herman, B. K., & Potenza, M. N. (2016). The neurobiological basis of binge-eating disorder. *Neuroscience and Biobehavioral Reviews*, *63*, 223–238. https://doi.org/10.1016/j.neubiorev.2016.01.013

Kremen, W. S., Koenen, K. C., Afari, N., & Lyons, M. J. Twin studies of posttraumatic stress disorder: Differentiating vulnerability factors from sequelae. (2012). *Neuropharmacology*, *62* (2), 647–653. 012. https://doi.org/10.1016/j.neuropharm.2011.03.012

Linnér, R. K., Mallard, T., Barr, P., Sanchez-Roige, S., Waldman, I., Palmer, A. A., ... Dick, D. M. (2020, January 13-14). *Using multivariate analyses to aid in gene identification: The externalizing consortium* [Paper presentation]. Genetics and Epigenetics Cross-Cutting Research Team, Rockville, MD, United Stated.

Loehlin, J. C. (1996). The Cholesky approach: A cautionary note. *Behavior Genetics*, *26*(1), 65–69. https://doi.org/10.1007/BF02361160

Magruder, K., Yeager, D., Goldberg, J., Forsberg, C., Litz, B., Vaccarino, V., Friedman, M., Gleason, T., Huang, G., & Smith, N. (2015). Diagnostic performance of the PTSD checklist and the Vietnam era twin registry PTSD scale. *Epidemiology and Psychiatric Sciences*, *24*(5), 415–422. https://doi.org/10.1017/S2045796014000365

Mason, J. E., LeBouthillier, D. M., & Asmundson, G. J. (2019). Relationships between health behaviors, posttraumatic stress disorder, and comorbid general anxiety and depression. *Cognitive Behaviour Therapy*, *48*(3), 184–199. https://doi.org/10.1080/16506073.2018.1498119

Mason, S. M., Frazier, P. A., Austin, S. B., Harlow, B. L., Jackson, B., Raymond, N. C., & Rich-Edwards, J. W. (2017). Posttraumatic stress disorder symptoms and problematic overeating behaviors in young men and women. *Annals of Behavioral Medicine*, *51*(6), 822–832. https://doi.org/10.1007/s12160-017-9905-1

McGue, M., & Bouchard, T., Jr. (1984). Adjustment of twin data for the effects of age and sex. *Behavior Genetics*, *14*(4), 325–343. https://doi.org/10.1007/BF01080045

Mitchell, K., Neale, M., Bulik, C., Aggen, S., Kendler, K., & Mazzeo, S. (2010). Binge eating disorder: A symptom-level investigation of genetic and environmental influences on liability. *Psychological Medicine*, *40*(11), 1899–1906. https://doi.org/10.1017/S0033291710000139

Mitchell, K. S., Mazzeo, S. E., Schlesinger, M. R., Brewerton, T. D., & Smith, B. N. (2012). Comorbidity of partial and subthreshold PTSD among men and women with eating disorders in the national comorbidity survey-replication study. *International Journal of Eating Disorders*, *45*(3), 307–315. https://doi.org/10.1002/eat.20965

National Center for PTSD. (n.d.). *Using the PTSD Checklist for DSM-IV (PCL)*. https://www.ptsd.va.gov/professional/assessment/documents/PCL_handoutDSM4.pdf

Neale, B. M., Mazzeo, S. E., & Bulik, C. M. (2003). A twin study of dietary restraint, disinhibition and hunger: An examination of the eating inventory (three factor eating questionnaire). *Twin Research and Human Genetics*, *6*(6), 471–478. https://doi.org/10.1375/136905203322686455

Neale, M. C., Hunter, M. D., Pritikin, J. N., Zahery, M., Brick, T. R., Kirkpatrick, R. M., Estabrook, R., Bates, T. C., Maes, H. H., & Boker, S. M. (2016). OpenMx 2.0: Extended structural equation and statistical modeling. *Psychometrika*, *81*(2), 535–549. https://doi.org/10.1007/s11336-014-9435-8

Neale, M. C., & Maes, H. H. M. (2004). *Methodology for genetic studies of twins and families*. Kluwer Academic Publisher.

Plomin, R., & Daniels, D. (2011). Why are children in the same family so different from one another? *International Journal of Epidemiology*, *40*(3), 563–582. https://doi.org/10.1093/ije/dyq148

Polivy, J., Herman, C. P., & Howard, K. I. (1988). The restraint scale: Assessment of dieting. In M. Hersen & A. S. Bellack (Eds.), *Dictionary of behavioral assessment techniques* (pp. 377–380). Pergamon Press.

R Core Team. (2016). *R: A language and environment for statistical computing*. https://www.R-project.org/.

Reyes-Rodríguez, M. L., Ann Von Holle, T., Thornton, L. M., Klump, K. L., Brandt, H., Crawford, S., ...& Jones, I. (2011). Post traumatic stress disorder in anorexia nervosa. *Psychosomatic Medicine*, *73*(6), 491.

Sadeh, N., Spielberg, J. M., & Hayes, J. P. (2018). Impulsive responding in threat and reward contexts as a function of PTSD symptoms and trait disinhibition. *Journal of Anxiety Disorders*, *53*, 76–84. https://doi.org/10.1016/j.janxdis.2017.11.001

Sadeh, N., Spielberg, J. M., Miller, M. W., Milberg, W. P., Salat, D. H., Amick, M. M., ... McGlinchey, R. E. (2015). Neurobiological indicators of disinhibition in posttraumatic stress disorder. *Human Brain Mapping*, *36*(8), 3076–3086. https://doi.org/10.1002/hbm.22829

Sartor, C. E., McCutcheon, V. V., Pommer, N. E., Nelson, E. C., Grant, J. D., Duncan, A. E., Waldron, M., Bucholz, K. K., Madden, P. A. F., & Heath, A. C. (2011). Common genetic and environmental contributions to post-traumatic stress disorder and alcohol dependence in young women. *Psychological Medicine*, *41*(7), 1497–1505. https://doi.org/10.1017/S0033291710002072

Scharff, A., Ortiz, S. N., Forrest, L. N., & Smith, A. R. (2019). Comparing the clinical presentation of eating disorder patients with and without trauma history and/or comorbid PTSD. *Eating Disorders*, 28(1), 1–15. https://doi.org/10.1080/10640266.2019.1642035

Schaumberg, K., & Anderson, D. (2016). Dietary restraint and weight loss as risk factors for eating pathology. *Eating Behaviors*, *23*, 97–103. https://doi.org/10.1016/j.eatbeh.2016.08.009

Schur, E., Noonan, C., Polivy, J., Goldberg, J., & Buchwald, D. (2009). Genetic and environmental influences on restrained eating behavior. *International Journal of Eating Disorders*, *42*(8), 765–772. https://doi.org/10.1002/eat.20734

Sheerin, C. M., Lind, M. J., Bountress, K. E., Nugent, N. R., & Amstadter, A. B. (2017). The genetics and epigenetics of PTSD: Overview, recent advances, and future directions. *Current Opinion in Psychology, 14*, 5–11. https://doi.org/10.1016/j.copsyc.2016.09.003

Sommer, J. L., Mota, N., & El-Gabalawy, R. (2018). Maladaptive eating in posttraumatic stress disorder: A population-based examination of typologies and medical condition correlates. *Journal of Traumatic Stress, 31*(5), 708–718. https://doi.org/10.1002/jts.22323

Stein, M. B., McQuaid, J. R., Pedrelli, P., Lenox, R., & McCahill, M. E. (2000). Posttraumatic stress disorder in the primary care medical setting. *General Hospital Psychiatry, 22*(4), 261–269.

Strachan, E., Hunt, C., Afari, N., Duncan, G., Noonan, C., Schur, E., Watson, N., Goldberg, J., & Buchwald, D. (2013). University of Washington twin registry: Poised for the next generation of twin research. *Twin Research and Human Genetics, 16*(1), 455–462. https://doi.org/10.1017/thg.2012.124

Stunkard, A. J., & Messick, S. (1985). The three-factor eating questionnaire to measure dietary restraint, disinhibition and hunger. *Journal of Psychosomatic Research, 29*(1), 71–83. https://doi.org/10.1016/0022-3999(85)90010-8

Talbot, L. S., Maguen, S., Epel, E. S., Metzler, T. J., & Neylan, T. C. (2013). Posttraumatic stress disorder is associated with emotional eating. *Journal of Traumatic Stress, 26*(4), 521–525. https://doi.org/10.1002/jts.21824

Thornton, L. M., Mazzeo, S. E., & Bulik, C. M. (2010). The Heritability of Eating Disorders: Methods and Current Findings. In R. Adan & W. Kaye (Eds.), *Behavioral Neurobiology of Eating Disorders. Current Topics in Behavioral Neurosciences,* vol 6. Berlin, Heidelberg: Springer. https://doi.org/10.1007/7854_2010_91

Thornton, L. M., Dellava, J. E., Root, T. L., Lichtenstein, P. & Bulik, C. M. (2011). Anorexia nervosa and generalized anxiety disorder: further explorations of the relation between anxiety and body mass index. *Journal of Anxiety Disorders, 25*(5), 727–730.

Trottier, K., & MacDonald, D. E. (2017). Update on psychological trauma, other severe adverse experiences and eating disorders: State of the research and future research directions. *Current Psychiatry Reports, 19*(8), 45. https://doi.org/10.1007/s11920-017-0806-6

Trottier, K., Monson, C. M., Wonderlich, S. A., & Olmsted, M. P. (2017). Initial findings from project recover: Overcoming co-occurring eating disorders and posttraumatic stress disorder through integrated treatment. *Journal of Traumatic Stress, 30*(2), 173–177. https://doi.org/10.1002/jts.22176

Trottier, K., Wonderlich, S. A., Monson, C. M., Crosby, R. D., & Olmsted, M. P. (2016). Investigating posttraumatic stress disorder as a psychological maintaining factor of eating disorders. *International Journal of Eating Disorders, 49*(5), 455–457. https://doi.org/10.1002/eat.22516

Vainik, U., Neseliler, S., Konstabel, K., Fellows, L. K., & Dagher, A. (2015). Eating traits questionnaires as a continuum of a single concept. Uncontrolled eating. *Appetite, 90*, 229–239. https://doi.org/10.1016/j.appet.2015.03.004

Van Strien, T., Frijters, J. E., Bergers, G. P., & Defares, P. B. (1986). The Dutch Eating Behavior Questionnaire (DEBQ) for assessment of restrained, emotional, and external eating behavior. *International Journal of Eating Disorders, 5*(2), 295–315. https://doi.org/10.1002/1098-108X(198602)5:2<295::AID-EAT2260050209>3.0.CO;2-T

Verhulst, B. (2017). A power calculator for the classical twin design. *Behavior Genetics, 47*(2), 255–261. https://doi.org/10.1007/s10519-016-9828-9

Von Lojewski, A., Boyd, C., Abraham, S., & Russell, J. (2012). Lifetime and recent DSM and ICD psychiatric comorbidity of inpatients engaging in different eating disorder behaviours. *Eating and Weight Disorders-Studies on Anorexia, Bulimia and Obesity, 17*(3), e185–e193. https://doi.org/10.1007/BF03325346

Weathers, F., Litz, B., Herman, D., Huska, J., & Keane, T. (1993, October). *The PTSD checklist: Reliability, validity and diagnostic utility* [Paper presentation]. Annual Meeting of the International Society for Traumatic Stress Studies, San Antonio, TX, United States.

Yeager, D. E., Magruder, K. M., Knapp, R. G., Nicholas, J. S., & Frueh, B. C. (2007). Performance characteristics of the posttraumatic stress disorder checklist and SPAN in Veterans Affairs primary care settings. *General Hospital Psychiatry*, *29*(4), 294–301. https://doi.org/10.1016/j.genhosppsych.2007.03.004

Intimate partner violence and muscularity-building behavior in latino sexual minority men

Alexandra D. Convertino, John P. Brady, William Grunewald, and Aaron J. Blashill

ABSTRACT

Intimate partner violence (IPV) has been associated with increased prevalence of eating disorders. In men, disordered eating is often related to the muscularized ideal. Sexual minority men (SMM; e.g., gay, bisexual, etc.) are at higher risk for eating disorders and Latino SMM may be at particularly high risk; however, IPV and eating pathology has yet to be examined in this population. Therefore, the aim of this study is to elucidate the association between IPV and muscularity-related dissatisfaction and muscularity-oriented behavior in Latino SMM. Participants were 81 Latino SMM. Thirty participants (37% of the sample) met the cutoff score for experiencing IPV in the past month. In bivariate analyses, IPV was associated with muscularity-oriented behavior, but not muscularity-related dissatisfaction. In multivariable analyses, IPV was negatively associated with muscularity-related dissatisfaction with a small effect size and positively associated with muscularity-oriented behavior with a large effect size. It may be that SMM engage in muscle building behavior to increase self-esteem, regulate affect, or better physically protect themselves from their abusive partner. Future research should investigate motivation for muscle building behavior in individuals experiencing IPV.

Sexual minority men (SMM; e.g., gay, bisexual) have increased risk for disordered eating behaviors, including disordered behaviors that are consistent with muscularity-building (Blashill & Safren, 2014; Calzo et al., 2017; Eik-Nes et al., 2018; Matthews-Ewald et al., 2014; Yean et al., 2013). Intimate partner violence (IPV) is one factor which may increase risk for body image disturbance. IPV has been positively associated with eating disorders among women (Bartlett et al., 2018; Bundock et al., 2013), but results have been inconsistent among men, likely due to a small number of studies. Of particular interest, Latino SMM may have elevated rates of disordered eating behavior as compared to non-Latino White SMM. A study by Blashill et al. (2017) found that Latino sexual minority adolescent boys were at greater risk of anabolic-androgenic steroid misuse than non-Hispanic White adolescent boys. Furthermore, higher rates of body image disturbance, a significant correlate of disordered eating, have been found among Latino SMM as compared to other groups of SMM and sexual minority women (Gonzales IV & Blashill, under review 2021). Therefore, Latino SMM may be a particularly vulnerable population to muscularity-oriented pathology. Thus, this study will examine the association of IPV with disordered eating behavior among Latino SMM.

Eating pathology in men

The pursuit of the "ideal" male form in Western culture often focuses on the pursuit of both muscularity and leanness which manifests as a higher drive for muscularity and lower drive for thinness in comparison with women (Yean et al., 2013). Drive for muscularity is often reflected in behaviors that increase muscularity such as manipulating dietary intake, excessive exercise, taking protein supplements, and misusing anabolic-androgenic steroids (McCreary, 2007), which could be considered on the spectrum of disordered body image-related behaviors. Indeed, prior research has found that drive for muscularity is positively associated with leanness-based disordered eating (Tod & Edwards, 2015) as well as muscularity-oriented disordered eating (Cooper et al., 2020; Murray et al., 2019).

Within men, SMM may be at particular risk for developing maladaptive eating behaviors. Previous research has shown that SMM are at elevated risk for body dissatisfaction (Frederick & Essayli, 2016; Yean et al., 2013), eating disorders (Feldman & Meyer, 2007), and anabolic-androgenic steroid misuse (Blashill et al., 2017; Blashill & Safren, 2014) as compared to heterosexual men. Drive for muscularity is also elevated in SMM as compared to heterosexual men (Eik-Nes et al., 2018; Yean et al., 2013). Therefore, drive for muscularity is a useful measure of muscularity-related forms of body image and eating pathology spectrum behaviors in SMM.

IPV and eating pathology

Prior research has linked IPV experiences with eating pathology. IPV was positively associated with thinness-based disordered eating in women when assessed as both lifetime IPV (Bundock et al., 2013) and IPV during the last year (Bartlett et al., 2018). In men, IPV has been linked to thinness-based disordered eating in some studies (Bartlett et al., 2018; Bundock et al., 2013; Thapa & Kelvin, 2017) but not others (Jonas et al., 2014; Romito et al., 2013). The association between IPV and muscularity-related dissatisfaction and muscularity-oriented behaviors has not yet been examined to our knowledge.

IPV may be associated with eating pathology through multiple mechanisms. Three potential theoretical mechanisms include affect regulation, self-esteem enhancement, and self-protection. For example, prior research in men has demonstrated that disordered eating behaviors, such as binge eating, are linked to emotional regulation difficulties and negative affect (Davis-Becker et al., 2014; Kukk & Akkermann, 2017; Lavender & Anderson, 2009). Furthermore, a qualitative study on IPV in women found that participants often reported using disordered eating as a method of regulating negative affect associated with IPV (Wong & Chang, 2016). Although there is a dearth of information on IPV and men's body image, men may also engage in altered eating patterns and compensatory muscularity-oriented behaviors for similar purposes of emotion regulation (e.g., exercise for emotion regulation benefits). In addition, men may attempt to improve their self-esteem by increasing muscularity since IPV is often associated with decreases in self-esteem (Oliffe et al., 2014). Alternatively, IPV is often bidirectional in same-gender relationships between men (Stanley et al., 2006) and one reported reason for engaging in IPV is self-defense (Oliffe et al., 2014); thus, SMM may also engage in muscularity-oriented behaviors to build muscle to better physically defend themselves. Therefore, IPV should be examined in its association with both muscularity-related dissatisfaction and muscularity-oriented behaviors.

Latino SMM, IPV, and eating pathology

While limited research has examined eating pathology at the intersections of gender, ethnicity, and sexual orientation, what research does exist suggests that Latino SMM may have elevated rates of disordered eating behavior as compared to non-Latino White SMM. Previous research has found elevated rates of eating pathology in Latino individuals as compared to White individuals, and SMM of any race/ethnicity as compared to heterosexual individuals (Austin et al., 2013; Thapa & Kelvin, 2017). Furthermore, a study by Blashill et al. (2017) found elevated rates of anabolic-androgenic steroid misuse in Latino sexual minority adolescent boys as compared to non-Hispanic White sexual minority boys and Latino heterosexual boys. Emerging research has found clinical levels of body dissatisfaction in roughly 50% of Latino SMM (Gonzales IV & Blashill, under review 2021), suggesting that this population may be at elevated risk for eating disorder pathology as compared to non-Latino White SMM.

The association between IPV and eating pathology in Latino men, and especially Latino SMM is relatively understudied. A prior study in adolescents found that exposure to dating violence in Latino boys was associated with greater odds of unhealthy weight control behaviors (i.e., fasting, diet pills, vomiting, and laxatives to lose or maintain weight) as opposed to their unexposed counterparts (Cha et al., 2016), but this study did not examine sexual orientation. There has only been a single study examining the association of eating pathology and IPV within a sample of Latino SMM. This study in New York City youth found that Hispanic ethnicity did not explain additional variance in a model examining the association between dating violence and unhealthy weight control behavior by gender and sexual orientation (Thapa & Kelvin, 2017); however, this study did not measure muscularity-oriented dissatisfaction or behaviors. To the best of our knowledge, the association of IPV and muscularity-oriented eating spectrum behaviors has not yet been examined among Latino SMM.

The current study

The current study built upon past research by examining the association between IPV and disordered body image-related variables among Latino SMM. Specifically, the association between experiences of IPV and muscularity-related dissatisfaction and muscularity-oriented behavior were explored. We hypothesized that IPV within the past month would be positively associated with increased muscularity-based dissatisfaction and behavior.

Method

Participants

Participants were 207 Latino SMM who participated in an online survey in April through June 2017. Nineteen participants were excluded because they completed less than half of the provided questions. Three validity check items (e.g., "For this question, please select 'Definitely Agree' as your answer") were included to detect invalid responders. Only participants that correctly responded to at least two of the three attention-check items were included in analyses. Thirty-seven participants were excluded in this manner. Seventy participants were excluded from analysis because they were missing data on IPV, resulting in a final analytic sample of 81 participants (see Table 1 for full demographics). Sensitivity analyses were also conducted imputing data for individuals who completed greater than 50% of the IPV items (i.e., individuals who completed 3 items; $N = 37$). Results with multiple imputation ($N = 118$) indicated a similar pattern and magnitude of results to the listwise deletion approach; therefore, the listwise deletion approach is presented for parsimony.

Participants were recruited through the lab's participant registry as well as through advertisements on Grindr, a dating application for SMM accessed through mobile phones. The inclusion criteria for the survey were as follows: (1) between 18 and 29 years old, (2) identify as a man, (3) either English or Spanish-speaking, (4) sexual minority (e.g., gay, bisexual, pansexual, etc.) identity and/or same-gender attraction, (5)

Table 1. Demographics of the analytic sample (n = 81).

Characteristic	
Age	M (SD)
	24.0 (3.3)
Sexual Orientation	N (%)
Gay	64 (79.0)
Bisexual	16 (19.8)
Pansexual	1 (1.2)
Sexual Attraction	52 (64.2)
Males Only	12 (17.3)
Mostly Attracted to Males	13 (16.0)
Equally Attracted to Males and Females	2 (2.5)
Mostly Attracted to Females	
Race	47 (58.0)
White	15 (18.5)
Black/African American	3 (3.7)
Native American/American Indian	2 (2.5)
Asian/Pacific Islander	13 (16)
Other	1 (1.2%)
Missing	

Hispanic/Latino ethnicity, and (6) residing in San Diego, California. Because the current study is a secondary data analysis and the parent study addressed sexual risk behaviors related to HIV acquisition in Hispanic/Latino sexual minority men, participants were excluded if they reported HIV seropositive status and were therefore not available for analyses within the current study.

Procedure

Participants from the lab registry of prior study participants were emailed information and a link to the pre-screen eligibility survey. If participants were recruited through Grindr advertisements, they provided their email addresses on an online form and subsequently emailed the pre-screen eligibility survey. To complete the pre-screener, participants were required to log in through Facebook to verify that they were residents of San Diego. All identifying information for the participants was erased upon data collection completion. Participants were informed that their IP addresses were collected in order to prevent participants from taking the survey multiple times for repeated compensation. Participants could select whether the survey would be administered in English (n = 149) or Spanish (n = 2).

Upon verification of eligibility via the pre-screener, participants completed an online consent form prior to completing the study survey. After participants completed the survey, they were directed to a separate webpage for inputting their name and email to receive compensation (a 10 USD Amazon.com gift card). Informed consent was obtained for all participants in the current study. All aspects of this study were approved by the San Diego State University Institutional Review Board.

Measures

Intimate partner violence

IPV was measured for the past month using the HITS (Hurt-Insult-Threaten-Scream) screening tool (Sherin et al., 1998). The HITS is a four-item measure assessing how frequently an individual's partner physically hurts, insults, threatens, or screams at them. The HITS uses a 5-point Likert scale (1 = Never; 5 = Frequently). There were three additional response options, which were: "Not Applicable (n/a)," "I Don't Know," and "Refused/Refuse to answer." The current study utilized a cutoff score of 11 for positive screen of IPV for the purposes of describing the sample, as this threshold has shown to have strong sensitivity and specificity (88% and 97%, respectively; Shakil et al., 2005). Since the HITS also produces a continuous score, we did not dichotomize for regression analyses. Prior research has shown that dichotomizing continuous predictors leads to a substantial loss of statistical power (Royston et al., 2006); therefore, we chose to retain the continuous score for the main analyses. The HITS has been validated in Spanish, as well as in samples of men, inclusive of SMM (Chen et al., 2007; Shakil et al., 2005). Internal consistency for this measure was $\alpha = .92$.

Drive for muscularity

Muscularity concerns were measured with the Drive for Muscularity Scale (DMS; McCreary, 2007). The DMS is a 15-item survey that measures dissatisfaction with one's musculature as well as muscle-building behaviors, with higher scores indicating a greater drive for muscularity. Each item is scored on a 6-point Likert-type scale (1 = Always; 6 = Never). The DMS yields a mean total score and two subscales; one that measures engagement in muscularity-oriented behaviors and one that measures muscularity-related dissatisfaction. The DMS has been validated for use with Spanish-speaking males (Escoto et al., 2013). Internal consistency for the muscularity-related dissatisfaction subscale was $\alpha = .83$. Internal consistency for the muscularity-oriented behaviors subscale was $\alpha = .82$.

Appearance evaluation

The Multidimensional Body-Self Relations Questionnaire-Appearance Evaluation subscale (MBSRQ-AE; Cash, 2000) was used to measure participants' body satisfaction. The MBSRQ-AE is a subscale of the MBSRQ that measures the respondent's level of satisfaction and/or dissatisfaction with their body. This subscale consists of 7-items measured on a 5-point Likert scale (1 = Definitely Disagree; 5 = Definitely Agree). Lower scores indicate more body dissatisfaction; higher scores indicate more body satisfaction. The MBSRQ-AE has been validated in Spanish (Roncero et al., 2015). Internal consistency for the MBSRQ-AE was $\alpha = .75$.

Depressive symptoms

The Personal Health Questionnaire Depression Scale (PHQ-8; Kroenke & Spitzer, 2002) was used to assess depressive symptoms. This scale consists of 8-items measured on a 4-point frequency scale (0 = Not at all; 3 = Nearly every day). The PHQ-8 is a widely used measure of depressive symptoms in both large clinical studies and population-based studies. Additionally, this scale has been validated in Spanish (Huang et al., 2006). Internal consistency for the PHQ-8 was $\alpha = .76$.

Sociodemographics

Demographic information, such as age, sexual orientation, sexual attraction, race, highest grade level, and income were collected.

Statistical analyses

Positive screen of IPV, frequencies of each form of IPV, and mean scores on the DMS subscales were calculated. Bivariate Pearson and point-biserial correlations were used to assess association between all study variables and to evaluate additional variables for inclusion as covariates. Depressive symptoms and appearance evaluation were significantly associated with IPV and muscularity-related dissatisfaction; age was significantly associated with muscularity-related dissatisfaction. Given that depression, body dissatisfaction, and age have been identified by previous research as robust covariates of drive for muscularity in men (Brennan et al., 2012; Schneider et al., 2016), and the correlations found in the current sample, these were added as covariates. Muscularity-related dissatisfaction was included as a covariate in the model assessing the association of IPV with muscularity-oriented behaviors because previous work has established evidence that muscularity-related dissatisfaction theoretically precedes engagement in muscularity-oriented behaviors (Tylka, 2011) Therefore, muscularity-related dissatisfaction is important to control for in this model to determine the association between muscularity-oriented behaviors and IPV independent from muscularity-related dissatisfaction. Data were analyzed for assumptions of linearity and multicollinearity and all assumptions were met.

Hierarchical multiple regression was conducted to determine whether IPV experiences explained significant variance in muscularity-related dissatisfaction. Depressive symptoms, age, and appearance evaluation were entered in Step 1 and IPV experiences—measured on the continuous scale—was entered in Step 2. Similarly, hierarchical multiple regression was conducted to determine whether IPV contributed significantly to muscularity-oriented behaviors. Depressive symptoms, age, muscularity-related dissatisfaction, and appearance evaluation were entered in Step 1 and the IPV experiences were entered in Step 2. Cohen's f^2 is presented as a measure of effect size with the following benchmarks noted by Cohen (1988): ≥ 0.02 is small, ≥ 0.15 is medium, and ≥ 0.35 is large.

Results

Of the 81 participants who completed the HITS in full, 30 participants screened positive for experiencing IPV (37.0%). Forty-nine participants (60.5%) endorsed experiencing at least one form of IPV in the past month. Thirty-three participants (40.7%) endorsed their partner physically hurting them, 43 participants (53.1%) endorsed their partner insulting or talking down to them, 33 participants (40.7%) endorsed their partner threatening them with harm, and 41 participants (50.6%) endorsed their partner screaming or cursing at them in the past month. Muscularity-related dissatisfaction ($M = 3.36$, $SD = 1.14$) and muscularity-oriented behavior ($M = 2.60$, $SD = 0.95$) scores were comparable to prior samples of SMM (DeBlaere & Brewster, 2017) and presumably heterosexual men (McCreary et al., 2004). Pearson bivariate correlations were calculated between IPV experiences ($M = 8.86$, $SD = 5.45$) and muscularity-related dissatisfaction ($r = -.12$, $p = .268$), muscularity-oriented behavior ($r = .54$, $p < .001$), age ($r = .11$, $p = .320$), appearance evaluation ($r = -.22$, $p = .048$), and depressive symptoms ($r = .26$, $p = .020$).

A hierarchical multiple regression model was utilized to assess the contribution of age, depressive symptoms, and appearance evaluation, as well as the

Table 2. Summary of hierarchical regression analysis for variables associated with muscularity-related dissatisfaction (n = 81).

	Unstandardized					
Variable	*B*	*SE*	95% CI	*β*	Cohen's f^2	*t*
Step 1						
Depressive Symptoms	0.05	0.03	[0.00, 0.10]	0.23	0.05	2.04*
Appearance Evaluation	−0.25	0.17	[−0.59, 0.09]	−0.16	0.03	−1.47
Age	−0.08	0.04	[−0.16, −0.01]	−0.24	0.07	−2.31*
R^2	.19					
Adj. R^2	.16					
F for Change in R^2	5.90**					
Step 2						
Depressive Symptoms	0.06	0.03	[0.01, 0.11]	0.28	0.08	2.48*
Appearance Evaluation	−0.31	0.17	[−0.65, 0.03]	−0.19	0.04	−1.79
Age	−0.07	0.04	[−0.14, 0.00]	−0.21	0.05	−1.96
Intimate Partner Violence	−0.05	0.02	[−0.09, 0.00]	−0.22	0.05	−2.01*
R^2	.23					
Adj. R^2	.19					
F for Change in R^2	4.04*					

* $p < .05$, ** $p < .01$, *** $p < .001$

Note. Cohen (1988) provides the following benchmarks for effect size for f^2: ≥ 0.02 is small, ≥ 0.15 is medium, and ≥ 0.35 is large.

Table 3. Summary of hierarchical regression analysis for variables associated with muscularity-oriented behavior (n = 81).

	Unstandardized					
Variable	*B*	*SE*	95% CI	*β*	Cohen's f^2	*t*
Step 1						
Depressive Symptoms	0.05	0.02	[0.01, 0.10]	0.28	0.07	2.30*
Appearance Evaluation	0.23	0.16	[−0.08, 0.53]	0.17	0.03	1.46
Age	0.04	0.03	[−0.03, 0.11]	0.14	0.02	1.20
Muscularity-Related Dissatisfaction	0.05	0.10	[−0.15, 0.25]	0.06	0.00	0.51
R^2	.09					
Adj. R^2	.04					
F for Change in R^2	1.85					
Step 2						
Depressive Symptoms	0.02	0.02	[−0.02, 0.06]	0.12	0.01	1.01
Appearance Evaluation	0.38	0.13	[0.12, 0.64]	0.29	0.11	2.90**
Age	0.02	0.03	[−0.04, 0.08]	0.07	0.01	0.71
Muscularity-Related Dissatisfaction	0.17	0.09	[0.00, 0.34]	0.20	0.05	1.94
Intimate Partner Violence	0.10	0.02	[0.07, 0.14]	0.59	0.48	5.98***
R^2	.38					
Adj. R^2	.34					
F for Change in R^2	35.70***					

* $p < .05$, ** $p < .01$, *** $p < .001$

Note. Cohen (1988) provides the following benchmarks for effect size for f^2: ≥ 0.02 is small, ≥ 0.15 is medium, and ≥ 0.35 is large.

unique contribution of IPV to muscularity-related dissatisfaction (see Table 2). In Step 1, the covariate-only model was significant. Step 2 was significant, demonstrated significant improvement over Step 1, and IPV experiences was negatively associated with muscularity-related dissatisfaction. Similarly, a hierarchical multiple regression model was utilized to assess the contribution of depressive symptoms, appearance evaluation, and muscularity-related dissatisfaction, as well as the unique contribution of IPV to muscularity-oriented behaviors (see Table 3). In Step 1, the covariate-only model was non-significant. Step 2 was significant, demonstrated significant improvement over Step 1, and IPV experiences were positively associated with muscularity-oriented behaviors.

Discussion

SMM endorse elevated rates of disordered eating (Feldman & Meyer, 2007), body dissatisfaction (Frederick & Essayli, 2016), and drive for muscularity (Eik-Nes et al., 2018; Yean et al., 2013) as compared to heterosexual men. Furthermore, there is some indication that Latino SMM may be at increased risk for disordered muscularity-oriented behaviors and clinical body image concerns, even in comparison to other groups of SMM (Eik-Nes et al., 2018; Gonzales IV & Blashill, under review 2021). IPV may be a potential explanatory factor for eating pathology in general and the specific muscularity-based behaviors that are characteristic of body image concerns in men (Murray et al.,

2017). To our knowledge, this is the first study to examine associations between experiences of IPV and muscularity-related dissatisfaction and muscularity-oriented behaviors in Latino SMM. Results of the study were that greater IPV displayed a small effect size with lower muscularity-related dissatisfaction in multivariable models; however, non-significant associations were revealed in bivariate models. Therefore, this finding should be interpreted with caution. In contrast, greater IPV was associated with increased muscularity-oriented behavior with a large effect size, both in bivariate and multivariable models. Age, depressive symptoms, muscularity-related dissatisfaction, and appearance evaluation are some of the most robust correlates of body change behaviors (Brennan et al., 2012; Schneider et al., 2016). Since IPV was associated with muscularity-oriented behavior even while controlling for these covariates, this finding suggests that there may be alternative motivations for engaging in muscle building behavior in Latino SMM that are experiencing IPV, beyond body dissatisfaction.

In the current sample, 37% of participants met the cutoff for experiencing IPV in the past month. For comparison, 5.2% of all men in the U.S. experienced IPV during the past 12 months in 2015 (Smith et al., 2018). Few prior studies have examined prevalence rates of IPV in Latino SMM. Of the studies that have examined Latino SMM, our sample endorsed greater rates of any abuse (61% versus 51–52%), psychological abuse (53% versus 33–45%) and physical abuse (41% versus 24–35%) in the past month than the lifetime rates found in these studies (Feldman et al., 2007; Nieves-Rosa et al., 2000; Toro-Alfonso & Rodríguez-Madera, 2004). Of note, it is unclear how the aforementioned studies handled missing data. Therefore, the estimates from this study may be higher than previously reported due to our exclusion of individuals that did not complete the HITS screening measure in full.

While little research has focused on physical protection strategies that SMM enact in response to IPV, it is possible that Latino SMM engage in muscle building behavior to physically protect themselves from their abusive partner. Prior research has found that sexual minority individuals endorse perpetrating IPV for self-defense or retaliation against prior violence (Donovan et al., 2014; Stanley et al., 2006). While the current study did not assess the perpetration of IPV or motives for muscularity building, it is possible that the men in our sample engaged in muscle building behavior to either avoid confrontations of violence or respond with violent means. Further research should be conducted in Latino SMM to determine the motivations behind muscularity-building behavior and whether this is related to the perpetration of or protection against IPV.

Alternatively, building muscle may serve to increase self-esteem and/or regulate negative affect after experiences of IPV. SMM often feel that their self-esteem needs to be rebuilt after IPV (Oliffe et al., 2014), and men anticipate an increase in confidence with greater muscularity (Frederick et al., 2007).

Therefore, SMM may pursue muscle building as a gender-consistent method of improving their physical appearance, and therefore self-esteem. In addition, exercise is often encouraged for its emotion regulation qualities and experimental studies have shown that exercise is effective for regulating anger, sadness, and anxiety (e.g., Bernstein & McNally, 2017). It is therefore plausible that SMM may engage in muscle building behaviors to modulate their feelings of self-blame, guilt, anger, or other negative affect after experiences of IPV.

The current study is not without limitations. The HITS screening measure only assesses IPV in the past month, does not assess for sexual abuse, nor does it assess for potential SMM-specific forms of abuse, such as forced "outing" of a partner. Motivations for engaging in muscularity-oriented behaviors were not assessed, which means that the association between IPV and muscularity-building behavior remains unexplained. Eating pathology assessment was limited; future research should consider assessing the association between IPV and muscularity-oriented eating pathology. The current study is cross-sectional in design, precluding any temporal ordering of variables. Furthermore, the sample was limited in scope, as data were collected from San Diego and may not generalize to Latino SMM outside of Southern California. Finally, the final analytic sample was small, and thus, caution should be taken in generalizing findings until replication occurs with a larger sample.

This study may impart certain clinical implications. IPV can be a traumatic event and prior research indicates that traumatic events and posttraumatic symptoms were more common in men with eating disorders than those without (Mitchell et al., 2012). Given the association of IPV and muscularity-oriented behaviors found in the current study, clinicians working with clients with muscularity-oriented behaviors should consider whether clients' prior or current experiences with IPV may be influencing and/or perpetuating their symptoms. This may require integrating trauma-informed care as indicated by clinical need (see Brewerton, 2019 for specific recommendations). Clinicians may consider the effect that trauma-related symptoms and experiences may have for their clients with muscularity-oriented behaviors in case formulations.

Another clinical implication is the importance of assessing for muscularity-related eating and behaviors in all individuals, but also specifically SMM that present to eating disorder treatment. Eating disorder assessment has traditionally only measured thinness-based pathology, which systematically under-identifies males with muscularity-focused eating pathology (Murray et al., 2017). The DMS (McCreary, 2007) used in this study may be of clinical utility, as well as the Muscularity Oriented Eating Test (Murray et al., 2019). Clinicians are encouraged to utilize assessment tools that specifically assess for muscularity-oriented behaviors to avoid missing relevant symptom targets for intervention.

In summary, the current study contributes to the literature by examining the association between IPV and muscularity dissatisfaction and behavior in Latino SMM. Results found that IPV is associated with greater muscularity-building behavior. Latino SMM may engage in muscularity-oriented behavior for increasing self-esteem, managing negative affect, or to physically defend themselves. Future research should investigate motivations for muscle-building behavior within the context of IPV. Results may be incorporated into clinical practice by integrating trauma-informed care into eating pathology treatment.

ORCID

Alexandra D. Convertino http://orcid.org/0000-0003-0073-6053

References

Austin, S. B., Nelson, L. A., Birkett, M. A., Calzo, J. P., & Everett, B. (2013). Eating disorder symptoms and obesity at the intersections of gender, ethnicity, and sexual orientation in US high school students. *American Journal of Public Health, 103*(2), e16–e22. https://doi.org/10.2105/AJPH.2012.301150

Bartlett, B. A., Iverson, K. M., & Mitchell, K. S. (2018). Intimate partner violence and disordered eating among male and female veterans. *Psychiatry Research, 260*, 98–104. https://doi.org/10.1016/j.psychres.2017.11.056

Bernstein, E. E., & McNally, R. J. (2017). Acute aerobic exercise helps overcome emotion regulation deficits. *Cognition and Emotion, 31*(4), 834–843. https://doi.org/10.1080/02699931.2016.1168284

Blashill, A. J., Calzo, J. P., Griffiths, S., & Murray, S. B. (2017). Anabolic steroid misuse among US adolescent boys: Disparities by sexual orientation and race/ethnicity. *American Journal of Public Health, 107*(2), 319–321. https://doi.org/10.2105/AJPH.2016.303566

Blashill, A. J., & Safren, S. A. (2014). Sexual orientation and anabolic-androgenic steroids in US adolescent boys. *Pediatrics, 133*(3), 469–475. https://doi.org/10.1542/peds.2013-2768

Brennan, D. J., Craig, S. L., & Thompson, D. E. A. (2012). Factors associated with a drive for muscularity among gay and bisexual men. *Culture, Health & Sexuality, 14*(1), 1–15. https://doi.org/10.1080/13691058.2011.619578

Brewerton, T. D. (2019). An overview of trauma-informed care and practice for eating disorders. *Journal of Aggression, Maltreatment & Trauma, 28*(4), 445–462. https://doi.org/10.1080/10926771.2018.1532940

Bundock, L., Howard, L. M., Trevillion, K., Malcolm, E., Feder, G., & Oram, S. (2013). Prevalence and risk of experiences of intimate partner violence among people with eating disorders: A systematic review. *Journal of Psychiatric Research, 47*(9), 1134–1142. https://doi.org/10.1016/j.jpsychires.2013.04.014

Calzo, J. P., Blashill, A. J., Brown, T. A., & Argenal, R. L. (2017). Eating disorders and disordered weight and shape control behaviors in sexual minority populations. *Current Psychiatry Reports, 19*(8), 49. https://doi.org/10.1007/s11920-017-0801-y

Cash, T. F. (2000). *The MBSRQ users' manual. Available from the author at www.body-Images.Com.*

Cha, S., Ihongbe, T. O., & Masho, S. W. (2016). Racial and gender differences in dating violence victimization and disordered eating among U.S. high schools. *Journal of Women's Health, 25* (8), 791–800. https://doi.org/10.1089/jwh.2015.5324

Chen, P.-H., Rovi, S., Washington, J., Jacobs, A., Vega, M., Pan, K.-Y., & Johnson, M. S. (2007). Randomized comparison of 3 methods to screen for domestic violence in family practice. *The Annals of Family Medicine, 5*(5), 430–435. https://doi.org/10.1370/afm.716

Cohen, J. (1988). *Statistical power analysis for the behavioral sciences* (2nd ed.). Lawrence Erlbaum Associates, Inc.

Cooper, M., Griffiths, K. M., & Burns, R. (2020). Getting shredded: Development and validation of a measure of muscularity-oriented disordered eating. *Psychological Assessment, 32*(5), 451–460. https://doi.org/10.1037/pas0000804

Davis-Becker, K., Peterson, C. M., & Fischer, S. (2014). The relationship of trait negative urgency and negative affect to disordered eating in men and women. *Personality and Individual Differences, 56*, 9–14. https://doi.org/10.1016/j.paid.2013.08.010

DeBlaere, C., & Brewster, M. E. (2017). A confirmation of the drive for muscularity scale with sexual minority men. *Psychology of Sexual Orientation and Gender Diversity, 4*(2), 227–232. https://doi.org/10.1037/sgd0000224

Donovan, C., Barnes, R., & Nixon, C. (2014). *The coral project: Exploring abusive behaviours in lesbian, gay, bisexual and/or transgender relationships (Interim Report)*. University of Sunderland and University of Leicester. https://www2.le.ac.uk/departments/criminology/documents/coral-project-interim-report

Eik-Nes, T. T., Austin, S. B., Blashill, A. J., Murray, S. B., & Calzo, J. P. (2018). Prospective health associations of drive for muscularity in young adult males. *International Journal of Eating Disorders, 51*(10), 1185–1193. https://doi.org/10.1002/eat.22943

Escoto, C., Alvarez-Rayón, G., Mancilla-Díaz, J. M., Camacho Ruiz, E. J., Franco Paredes, K., & Juárez Lugo, C. S. (2013). Psychometric properties of the drive for muscularity scale in Mexican males. *Eating and Weight Disorders, 18*(1), 23–28. https://doi.org/10.1007/s40519-013-0010-6

Feldman, M. B., Díaz, R. M., Ream, G. L., & El-Bassel, N. (2007). Intimate partner violence and HIV sexual risk behavior among Latino gay and bisexual men. *Journal of LGBT Health Research, 3*(2), 9–19. https://doi.org/10.1300/J463v03n02_02

Feldman, M. B., & Meyer, I. H. (2007). Eating disorders in diverse lesbian, gay, and bisexual populations. *International Journal of Eating Disorders, 40*(3), 218–226. https://doi.org/10.1002/eat.20360

Frederick, D. A., Buchanan, G. M., Sadehgi-Azar, L., Peplau, L. A., Haselton, M. G., Berezovskaya, A., & Lipinski, R. E. (2007). Desiring the muscular ideal: Men's body satisfaction in the United States, Ukraine, and Ghana. *Psychology of Men & Masculinity, 8* (2), 103–117. https://doi.org/10.1037/1524-9220.8.2.103

Frederick, D. A., & Essayli, J. H. (2016). Male body image: The roles of sexual orientation and body mass index across five national U.S. Studies. *Psychology of Men & Masculinity, 17*(4), 336–351. https://doi.org/10.1037/men0000031

Gonzales, M., IV, & Blashill, A. J. (under review 2021). Ethnic/racial and gender differences in body image disorders among a diverse sample of sexual minority U.S. adults. *Body Image*, 36, 64–73. https://doi.org/10.1016/j.bodyim.2020.10.007

Huang, F. Y., Chung, H., Kroenke, K., Delucchi, K. L., & Spitzer, R. L. (2006). Using the patient health questionnaire-9 to measure depression among racially and ethnically diverse primary care patients. *Journal of General Internal Medicine, 21*(6), 547–552. https://doi.org/10.1111/j.1525-1497.2006.00409.x

Jonas, S., Khalifeh, H., Bebbington, P. E., McManus, S., Brugha, T., Meltzer, H., & Howard, L. M. (2014). Gender differences in intimate partner violence and psychiatric disorders in England: Results from the 2007 adult psychiatric morbidity survey. *Epidemiology and Psychiatric Sciences*, *23*(2), 189–199. https://doi.org/10.1017/S2045796013000292

Kroenke, K., & Spitzer, R. L. (2002). The PHQ-9: A new depression diagnostic and severity measure. *Psychiatric Annals*, *32*(9), 509–515. https://doi.org/10.3928/0048-5713-20020901-06

Kukk, K., & Akkermann, K. (2017). Fluctuations in negative emotions predict binge eating both in women and men: An experience sampling study. *Eating Disorders*, *25*(1), 65–79. https://doi.org/10.1080/10640266.2016.1241058

Lavender, J. M., & Anderson, D. A. (2009). Contribution of emotion regulation difficulties to disordered eating and body dissatisfaction in college men. *International Journal of Eating Disorders*, 43(4), 352-357. https://doi.org/10.1002/eat.20705

Matthews-Ewald, M. R., Zullig, K. J., & Ward, R. M. (2014). Sexual orientation and disordered eating behaviors among self-identified male and female college students. *Eating Behaviors*, *15*(3), 441–444. https://doi.org/10.1016/j.eatbeh.2014.05.002

McCreary, D. R. (2007). The drive for muscularity scale: Description, psychometrics, and research findings. In J. K. Thompson & G. Cafri (Eds.), *The muscular ideal: Psychological, social, and medical perspectives* (pp. 87–106). American Psychological Association.

McCreary, D. R., Sasse, D. K., Saucier, D. M., & Dorsch, K. D. (2004). Measuring the drive for muscularity: Factorial validity of the drive for muscularity scale in men and women. *Psychology of Men & Masculinity*, *5*(1), 49–58. https://doi.org/10.1037/1524-9220.5.1.49

Mitchell, K. S., Mazzeo, S. E., Schlesinger, M. R., Brewerton, T. D., & Smith, B. N. (2012). Comorbidity of partial and subthreshold PTSD among men and women with eating disorders in the National comorbidity survey-replication study: PTSD and eating disorders in men and women. *International Journal of Eating Disorders*, *45*(3), 307–315. https://doi.org/10.1002/eat.20965

Murray, S. B., Brown, T. A., Blashill, A. J., Compte, E. J., Lavender, J. M., Mitchison, D., Mond, J. M., Keel, P. K., & Nagata, J. M. (2019). The development and validation of the muscularity-oriented eating test: A novel measure of muscularity-oriented disordered eating. *International Journal of Eating Disorders*, *52*(12), 1389–1398. https://doi.org/10.1002/eat.23144

Murray, S. B., Nagata, J. M., Griffiths, S., Calzo, J. P., Brown, T. A., Mitchison, D., Blashill, A. J., & Mond, J. M. (2017). The enigma of male eating disorders: A critical review and synthesis. *Clinical Psychology Review*, *57*, 1–11. https://doi.org/10.1016/j.cpr.2017.08.001

Nieves-Rosa, L. E., Carballo-Dieguez, A., & Dolezal, C. (2000). Domestic abuse and HIV-risk behavior in Latin American men who have sex with men in New York City. *Journal of Gay & Lesbian Social Services*, *11*(1), 77–90. https://doi.org/10.1300/J041v11n01_04

Oliffe, J. L., Han, C., Maria, E. S., Lohan, M., Howard, T., Stewart, D. E., & MacMillan, H. (2014). Gay men and intimate partner violence: A gender analysis. *Sociology of Health & Illness*, *36*(4), 564–579. https://doi.org/10.1111/1467-9566.12099

Romito, P., Beltramini, L., & Escribà-Agüir, V. (2013). Intimate partner violence and mental health among Italian adolescents: Gender similarities and differences. *Violence Against Women*, *19*(1), 89–106. https://doi.org/10.1177/1077801212475339

Roncero, M., Perpiñá, C., Marco, J. H., & Sánchez-Reales, S. (2015). Confirmatory factor analysis and psychometric properties of the Spanish version of the multidimensional body-self relations questionnaire-appearance scales. *Body Image*, *14*, 47–53. https://doi.org/10.1016/j.bodyim.2015.03.005

Royston, P., Altman, D. G., & Sauerbrei, W. (2006). Dichotomizing continuous predictors in multiple regression: A bad idea. *Statistics in Medicine*, *25*(1), 127–141. https://doi.org/10.1002/sim.2331

Schneider, C., Rollitz, L., Voracek, M., & Hennig-Fast, K. (2016). Biological, psychological, and sociocultural factors contributing to the drive for muscularity in weight-training men. *Frontiers in Psychology, 7*, 1992. https://doi.org/10.3389/fpsyg.2016.01992

Shakil, A., Donald, S., Sinacore, J. M., & Krepcho, M. (2005). Validation of the HITS domestic violence screening tool with males. *Family Medicine, 37*(3), 193–198. http://www.stfm.org/fmhub/fm2005/March/Amer193.pdf

Sherin, K. M., Sinacore, J. M., Li, X. Q., Zitter, R. E., & Shakil, A. (1998). HITS: A short domestic violence screening tool for use in a family practice setting. *Family Medicine, 30*(7), 508–512.

Smith, S. G., Zhang, X., Basile, K. C., Merrick, M. T., Wang, J., Kresnow, M., & Chen, J. (2018). *The National intimate partner and sexual violence survey (NISVS): 2015 data brief – updated release.* National Center for Injury Prevention and Control, Centers for Disease Control and Prevention.

Stanley, J. L., Bartholomew, K., Taylor, T., Oram, D., & Landolt, M. (2006). Intimate violence in male same-sex relationships. *Journal of Family Violence, 21*(1), 31–41. https://doi.org/10.1007/s10896-005-9008-9

Thapa, K., & Kelvin, E. A. (2017). Peer victimization and unhealthy weight control behaviors—the role of intersecting identities among New York City youth. *Journal of Urban Health, 94*(4), 506–513. https://doi.org/10.1007/s11524-017-0163-0

Tod, D., & Edwards, C. (2015). A meta-analysis of the drive for muscularity's relationships with exercise behaviour, disordered eating, supplement consumption, and exercise dependence. *International Review of Sport and Exercise Psychology, 8*(1), 185–203. https://doi.org/10.1080/1750984X.2015.1052089

Toro-Alfonso, J., & Rodríguez-Madera, S. (2004). Domestic violence in Puerto Rican gay male couples: Perceived prevalence, intergenerational violence, addictive behaviors, and conflict resolution skills. *Journal of Interpersonal Violence, 19*(6), 639–654. https://doi.org/10.1177/0886260504263873

Tylka, T. L. (2011). Refinement of the tripartite influence model for men: Dual body image pathways to body change behaviors. *Body Image, 8*(3), 199–207. https://doi.org/10.1016/j.bodyim.2011.04.008

Wong, S. P. Y., & Chang, J. C. (2016). Altered eating behaviors in female victims of intimate partner violence. *Journal of Interpersonal Violence, 31*(20), 3490–3505. https://doi.org/10.1177/0886260515585535

Yean, C., Benau, E. M., Dakanalis, A., Hormes, J. M., Perone, J., & Timko, C. A. (2013). The relationship of sex and sexual orientation to self-esteem, body shape satisfaction, and eating disorder symptomatology. *Frontiers in Psychology, 4, 887*. https://doi.org/10.3389/fpsyg.2013.00887

Part II

Mechanisms of effect

Understanding relationships between posttraumatic stress disorder symptoms, binge-eating symptoms, and obesity-related quality of life: the role of experiential avoidance

Jennalee S. Wooldridge, Matthew S. Herbert, Cara Dochat, and Niloofar Afari

ABSTRACT

Obesity, binge-eating symptoms, and PTSD symptoms commonly co-occur. Avoidance, a key feature of PTSD and proposed mechanism of binge-eating, is one potential mechanism for explaining this clinical overlap. The purpose of the current study was to: 1) examine the associations between PTSD symptoms (PTSD Checklist-Civilian; PCL-C) and measures of binge eating symptoms (Binge Eating Scale; BES) and obesity-related quality of life (Obesity Related Well-Being Questionnaire-97; ORWELL-97) in a sample of veterans with overweight or obesity ($N = 89$), and 2) determine whether experiential avoidance (The Acceptance and Action Questionnaire–II; AAQ-II) explains the relationship between PTSD symptoms and binge-eating symptoms, and PTSD symptoms and obesity-related quality of life, respectively. Scores on the PCL-C, BES, ORWELL-97, and AAQ-II were all significantly correlated. Linear regression analyses indicated that higher PCL-C scores were related to higher scores on the BES and ORWELL-97 after controlling for potentially confounding factors (BMI and race). Effect sizes were in the medium-large range. Further, AAQ-II mediated the relationship between PCL-C and ORWELL-97, but did not mediate the relationship between PCL-C and BES. These findings suggest that experiential avoidance should be considered in interventions addressing co-occurring PTSD, binge-eating, and poor obesity-related well-being. Longitudinal research is needed to better understand directionality of these relationships and changes over time.

Clinical Implications

- PTSD symptoms were positively related to binge-eating symptoms
- PTSD symptoms were related to worse obesity-related quality of life

- Avoidance explained the relationship between PTSD symptoms and quality of life
- Targeting avoidance may reduce PTSD symptoms and improve quality of life
- Tailored interventions for treating comorbid eating and trauma concerns are needed

Obesity is a global epidemic related to higher health care costs (Biener et al., 2017; Jia & Lubetkin, 2005) and poor health outcomes (Dixon, 2010). Additionally, individuals with obesity experience physical discomfort, impaired social functioning, and psychological distress, which in turn is associated with poor quality of life (Albano et al., 2019; Mannucci et al., 1999; De Zwaan et al., 2002). Among adults with overweight and obesity, binge-eating symptoms are common and can impede weight-loss efforts and increase the probability of weight (re)gain (Bertoli et al., 2016; Masheb et al., 2015). This relationship is particularly relevant for military veterans who access health care Through the Veterans Healthcare Administration, who experience a higher rate of obesity than the general U.S. population (Breland et al., 2017). Prior studies have reported that 22% of Veterans endorsed experiencing two or more episodes of bingeeating per week and 26% of Veterans have endorsed feeling a loss of control around eating (Dorflinger et al., 2017; Higgins et al., 2013; Slane et al., 2016).

Posttraumatic stress disorder (PTSD) is also prevalent among military veterans (Fulton et al., 2015; Kang, 2003; Marmar et al., 2015). In both veteran (Bartoli et al., 2015; Higgins et al., 2013; Litwack et al., 2014; Smith et al., 2015; Vieweg et al., 2007) and civilian samples (Brewerton, 2007; Mitchell et al., 2012), PTSD frequently co-occurs with obesity and binge-eating (Mason et al., 2017). It has been hypothesized that experiencing trauma, in combination with pre-existing shared biological and emotional dysregulation, makes some individuals more susceptible to both disordered eating and PTSD (Mitchell et al., 2012). Additionally, individuals with PTSD may use food to cope with negative affect and stress, leading to the development of unhealthy eating habits and obesity (Mason et al., 2017; Scott et al., 2008; Talbot et al., 2013). However, mechanisms explaining the relationship between binge-eating symptoms, obesity-related quality of life, and PTSD symptoms among veterans with overweight and obesity have not been explicitly examined. It is essential to understand the psychological processes underlying these commonly co-occurring broader symptomologies, as they are related to poorer physical and mental health outcomes (Hall et al., 2015; Higgins et al., 2013), and could potentially be treated simultaneously. Further, eating and weight concerns are common among male veterans (Rosenberger & Dorflinger, 2013), but men are typically underrepresented in eating disorder research

(Rosenberger & Dorflinger, 2013; Valente et al., 2017), indicating a need for understanding mechanisms in men in particular.

Experiential avoidance, or the unwillingness to experience unpleasant thoughts, emotions, and memories, may partly explain the relationship between PTSD symptoms and binge-eating symptoms and between PTSD symptoms and obesity-related quality of life. Experiential avoidance is a compelling candidate mechanism since avoidance behaviors are a key feature of PTSD (American Psychiatric Association, 2013) and play an important role in binge-eating. In terms of PTSD, avoidance behaviors are related to the development of PTSD, as well as functional impairment (Solomon & Mikulincer, 2007) and poor quality of life in persons with PTSD (Kashdan et al., 2009). In a study utilizing ecological momentary assessment among individuals with PTSD, avoidance was the most commonly used emotion regulation strategy among participants, and predicted subsequent increases in PTSD symptom severity (Short et al., 2018).

Bingeeating is well-documented as a means to avoid experiencing unpleasant and unwanted emotions, such as anxiety, depression, or boredom and thoughts (Allison et al., 2005; Barnes & Tantleff-Dunn, 2010; Lillis, Hayes et al., 2011). For example, experiential avoidance mediated the relationship between negative emotions and emotional eating among college students (Weineland et al., 2013). In adults with obesity seeking weight-loss treatment, experiential avoidance was associated with poorer health-related quality of life and mediated the relationship between body mass index (BMI) and health-related quality of life (Lillis, Levin et al., 2011). Further, treatments for binge-eating and weight-loss addressing experiential avoidance have demonstrated improvements in BMI, weight-related self-stigma, binge-eating, and physical activity levels (Lillis et al., 2009; Lillis, Hayes et al., 2011; Tapper et al., 2009). Thus, it is plausible that binge-eating behaviors function as a means to avoid unwanted symptoms of PTSD, such as hyperarousal, fear, and flashbacks. We are not aware of any studies that consider experiential avoidance in the context of obesity, binge-eating symptoms, and PTSD symptoms. However, in a sample of 71 persons with history of sexual trauma and 25 controls with no history of sexual trauma, Holzer et al. (2008) found preliminary support that avoidance symptoms mediate the association between sexual trauma history and eating disorder symptoms.

Given that experiential avoidance relates to PTSD symptoms and binge-eating symptoms, we posit that avoidance may explain the relationship between PTSD symptoms and binge-eating symptoms, as well as the relationships between PTSD symptoms and obesity-related quality of life, among veterans with overweight/obesity. Understanding common underlying psychological processes among these co-occurring concerns may inform the development of treatments that address these concerns simultaneously

(Brewerton, 2007). Thus, the purpose of the current study was to 1) examine the associations among PTSD symptoms and measures of binge-eating symptoms and obesity-related quality of life in a primarily male sample of veterans with overweight or obesity; and 2) determine whether experiential avoidance explains the relationship among PTSD symptoms and (a) binge-eating symptoms and (b) obesity-related quality of life.We hypothesized that 1) greater PTSD symptoms would be related to greater binge-eating symptoms and lower obesity-related quality of life, and 2) experiential avoidance would mediate the relationship between PTSD symptoms and (a) binge-eating symptoms and (b) obesity-related quality of life.

Method

Participants

Participants (N = 89, n_{male} = 67) were U.S. military veterans recruited for a clinical trial comparing Acceptance and Commitment Therapy (ACT) to behavioral weight loss to treat problematic eating (Afari et al., 2019). Problematic eating included a range of disinhibited eating behaviors including objective bingeeating, subjective bingeeating, overeating, loss of control eating, and emotional eating. Eligible participants had previously participated in *MOVE*©, the Veteran Health Administration's evidence-based, multidisciplinary weight management and health promotion program. Inclusion criteria for the original study and this secondary analysis were: aged 18–75 years, BMI ≥ 25 kg/m^2, participation in at least 5 of 8 *MOVE!* © sessions, and self-endorsement of problems with stress-related eating. Those with serious or unstable medical or psychiatric illness (i.e., history of active psychosis, current substance use disorder, anorexia nervosa, and bulimia nervosa), psychosocial instability (e.g., homelessness), conditions in which exercise or weight loss could be detrimental to health, current suicidality, previous experience with ACT, or currently participating in other interventions for obesity or binge eating were excluded. Potential participants were screened by telephone using the Mini International Neuropsychiatric Interview (Lecrubier et al., 1997). Measures collected at baseline from the clinical trial were used in the current study. The local Institutional Review Board and the Research and Development Committee approved the study. Informed consent was obtained from participants.

Measures

Demographic variables

Participants reported demographic characteristics including age, sex, race, ethnicity, education, and income at baseline.

Body mass index (BMI)

BMI (kg/m^2) was calculated using weight and height assessed by research staff.

Binge-eating symptoms

Binge-eating symptoms were assessed using the Binge Eating Scale (BES; Gormally et al., 1982). The BES is a 16-item self-report measure that assesses the behavioral, cognitive, and emotional features of bingeeating in adults with overweight and obesity. Participants are instructed to select one statement out of four that best describes their binge-eating-related attitudes and behaviors, from 16 groups of questions. Each statement is weighted either 0, 1, 2, or 3, and weights are summed for a total score. An example item weighted 0 is, "I rarely eat so much food that I feel uncomfortably stuffed afterward." An example item weighted 3 from the same group of statements is, "I eat so much food that I regularly feel quite uncomfortable after eating and sometimes a bit nauseous." Higher scores indicate greater bingeeating. The BES has good internal consistency and test-retest reliability in overweight and obese individuals (Gormally et al., 1982). A score of 18 or higher indicates clinically significant binge-eating (Greeno et al., 1995). Internal consistency in the current sample was excellent (Cronbach's alpha = .90)

Obesity-related quality of life

The Obesity-Related Well-Being Questionnaire-97 (ORWELL-97; Mannucci et al., 1999) is an 18-item self-report instrument designed to assess quality of life among persons with obesity in the domains of physical symptoms, physical discomfort, and familial, social, and occupational functioning. Respondents rate the frequency and severity of symptoms, and the extent to which certain domains are important and are limited due to obesity, on a 4-point scale from 0 (*not at all*) to 3 (*much*). Example items include, "Does shortness of breath represent an obstacle for your daily activities?" and "How important is it for you to exercise regularly?" The ORWELL-97 is scored by multiplying participants' subjective importance rating of each domain with the frequency of distress rating for each domain. Higher scores indicate lower quality of life. Internal consistency in the current sample was good (Cronbach's alpha = .88)

PTSD symptoms

The PTSD Checklist-Civilian (PCL-C; Blanchard et al., 1996) is a 17-item self-report measure used to assess PTSD symptoms caused by any traumatic event. This version simplifies assessment in the context of multiple traumatic events because symptom endorsements are attributed to "stressful experiences" rather than a specific event. Respondents indicate on a 5-point scale how bothered they have been by symptoms of PTSD over the past month from 1 (*not at all*) to 5 (*extremely*). Example items include, "Repeated, disturbing dreams of a stressful experience from the past," and "Feeling jumpy or easily startled." Items are summed to form a total score, with higher scores indicating greater PTSD symptom severity. Internal consistency in the current sample was excellent (Cronbach's alpha = .96)

Experiential avoidance

The Acceptance and Action Questionnaire–II (AAQ-II; Bond et al., 2011) is a 7-item self-report scale that assesses response to difficult thoughts, feelings, and physiological sensations. Participants rate the accuracy of statements on a 7-point scale from 1 (*never true*) to 7 (*always true*). Example items include, "Emotions cause problems in my life" and "I worry about not being able to control my worries and feelings." Higher scores indicate greater experiential avoidance. Internal consistency in the current sample was excellent (Cronbach's alpha = .95)

Data analyses

All analyses were conducted using IBM SPSS Statistics, version 26 (IBM Corp., Armonk, NY, USA). Bivariate correlations were used to examine relationships among PTSD symptoms (PCL-C), binge-eating symptoms (BES), obesity-related quality of life (ORWELL-97), and experiential avoidance (AAQ-II). Bivariate correlations and independent samples *t*-tests were used to identify potential demographic covariates. To address aim 1, separate hierarchical linear regression models were used to examine relationships between PTSD symptoms (independent variable) with binge-eating symptoms (outcome) and obesity-related quality of life (outcome), respectively. For each model, demographic covariates that were significantly related to outcome variables (i.e., BMI and race) were entered on the first step, and PCL-C score was entered on the second step. Analyses included cases that were randomized to treatment with complete data at baseline; therefore, there were no missing data in the present analyses. To address aim 2, separate cross-sectional mediation models were employed using the program for simple mediation from the PROCESS macro for SPSS (Preacher & Hayes, 2004) to examine whether experiential avoidance explains the relationship between PTSD symptoms and each outcome (binge-eating symptoms, obesity-related quality of life). PROCESS uses bootstrapping, a non-parametric resampling procedure, to estimate the indirect effects and generate confidence intervals (CI). The mediation effect is considered significant if the 95% CI does not include zero. Bootstrapping can be appropriate for small samples, does not make assumptions about the distribution of the sample, and decreases the chance of both type I and type II errors (Preacher & Hayes, 2004). Each analysis used 10,000 bootstrapped samples. Mediation models controlled for BMI and race. We also conducted sensitivity analyses using data from male participants only (n = 67) for each regression and mediation analysis.

Results

The average age of the sample was 55.97 years (SD = 10.86). The majority of participants were male (77.5%) and identified as White (68.5%). On average, participants' BMI (M = 37.5 m/kg^2, SD = 7.3) fell within the category of class 2 obesity (Centers for Disease Control and Prevention (CDC), 2017), which corresponds to BMIs between 35 and 40 m/kg^2, and is associated with a moderaterisk of obesity-related health risks (Jensen, 2016). Of the whole sample, 42% were married or cohabitating; 41% completed a bachelor's degree or higher education; 45% met the threshold for clinically significant binge-eating symptoms on the BES as proposed by Greeno et al. (1995), and 34% met criteria for PTSD at the time of the study per structured diagnostic interview. White participants had significantly higher BES scores [$t(87) = 2.14$, $p = .04$] than non-white participants. Higher BMI was related to higher ORWELL-97 scores ($r = .34$, $p = .001$). No other potential covariates were significantly related to study outcome variables.

Correlations, means, and standard deviations for study variables are presented in Table 1. Scores on the PCL-C, BES, ORWELL- 97, and AAQ-II were all significantly positively correlated. Hierarchical linear regression analyses indicated that higher PCL-C scores were related to higher scores on the BES and ORWEL-97, after controlling for BMI and race (see Table 2). Effect sizes

Table 1. Bivariate correlations, means, and standard deviations of study variables.

Measure	1.	2.	3.	4.	*M (SD)*	Range
1. PCL-C	-				34.10 (15.09)	17–79
2. AAQ-II	.67*	-			19.94 (10.58)	7–49
3. BES	.43*	.46*	-		16.34 (8.87)	0–38
4. ORWELL-97	.39*	.48*	.48*	-	49.58 (29.20)	2–138

Note. PCL-C = PTSD Checklist-Civilian, AAQ-II = Acceptance and Action Questionnaire–II, BES = Binge Eating Scale, ORWELL-97 = Obesity-Related Well-Being Questionnaire-97, *M* = Mean, *SD* = Standard deviation.
*p <.001

Table 2. Hierarchical linear regression analyses with PTSD symptoms predicting binge-eating symptoms and weight-related quality of life.

	BES				ORWELL-97			
Variable	*B*	*SE B*	*β*	95% CI	*B*	*SE B*	*β*	95% CI
1.								
BMI	.12	.13	.10	−.13,.38	1.35**	.41	.34	.53, 2.16
Ethnicity	−4.42*	2.03	−.23	−8.46, −.38	−8.06	6.43	−.13	−20.85, 4.73
2.								
BMI	.13	.12	.11	−.10,.36	1.36**	.37	.34	.63, 2.10
Ethnicity	−4.66*	1.82	−.24	−8.29, −1.04	−8.81	5.81	−.14	−20.36, 2.74
PCL-C	.26**	.06	.44	.15,.37	.80**	.18	.41	.44, 1.15
R^2	.51				.55			
F	9.47**				11.81**			

Note. *B* = Unstandardized beta, *SE B* = Standard Error of beta, *β* = Standardized coefficient Beta, CI = Confidence Interval, BES = Binge Eating Scale, ORWELL-97 = The Obesity-Related Well-Being Questionnaire-97, BMI = Body mass index, PCL-C = PTSD Checklist-Civilian.
* p <.05 ** p <.001

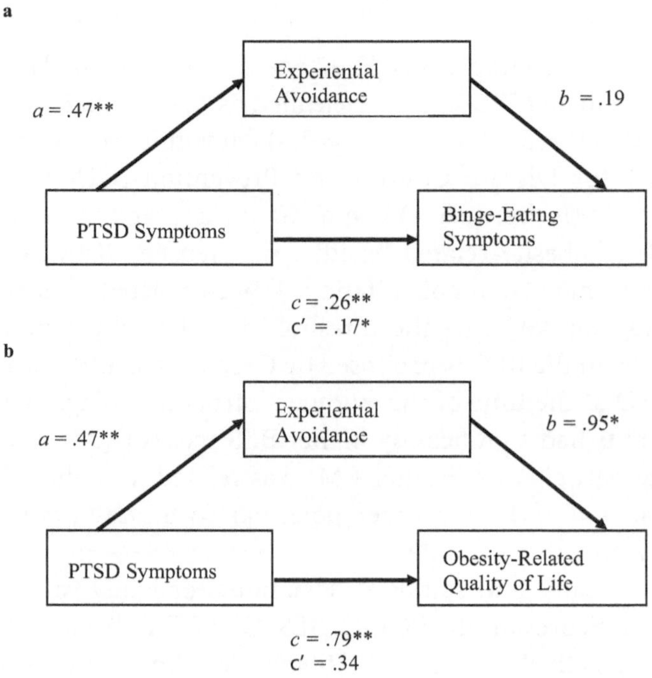

Figure 1. Coefficients for mediation models for binge-eating symptoms and obesity-related quality of life. *Note.* Model A shows the relationship between PTSD symptoms and binge-eating symptoms mediated by experiential avoidance. Model B shows the relationship between PTSD symptoms and obesity-related quality of life mediated by experiential avoidance. The paths *a, b, c* (total effect), and *c′* (direct effect) are unstandardized regression coefficients. $N = 87$, Ethnicity and BMI were included as covariates for all models. * $p < .05$, ** $p < .0001$

were in the medium-large range for the BES ($R^2 = .25$) and ORWELL-97 ($R^2 = .30$).

Mediation analyses

Results of the mediation analyses are presented in Figure 1.

Binge-eating symptoms

The total effect, which is the association between PCL-C and BES scores without taking AAQ-II into account (path c), was significant ($b = .26$, SE = .06, $t = 4.69$, $p < .001$, [95% CI: .15, .37]). There was also a significant direct association between PCL-C and BES scores when taking AAQ-II scores into account (path c') ($b = .17$, SE = .07, $t = 2.24$, $p = .03$, [95% CI: .02, .32]). The path between PCL-C and AAQ-II scores (path a) was significant and positive ($b = .47$, SE = .05, $t = 8.65$, $p < .001$, [95% CI: .15, .37]). The path between AAQ-II and BES scores was not significant (path b), ($b = .19$, SE = .11, $t = 1.79$, $p = .08$ [95% CI: −.02, .41]). The indirect association between PCL-C and BES scores through AAQ-II was not significant (B = .09, SE = .06, [95% CI:

−.03, .20]), indicating that AAQ-II scores did not mediate the relationship between PCL-C and BES scores.

Obesity-related quality of life

The total effect between PCL-C and ORWELL-97 scores was significant (path c) (b = .79, SE = .18, t = 4.47, p < .001, [95% CI: 44, 1.13]). The direct association between PCL-C and ORWELL-97 was not significant (path c') (b = .34., SE = .23, t = 1.45, p = .15, [95% CI: −.12, .80]). The path between PCL-C and AAQ-II scores was significant and positive (path a) (b = .47., SE = .05, t = 8.65, p < .001, [95% CI: .36, .58]). The path between AAQ-II and ORWELL-97 scores was significant and positive (path b) (b = .95, SE = .33, t = 2.84, p = .006, [95% CI: .29, 1.62]). The indirect association between PCL-C and ORWELL-97 scores was significant (B = .45, SE = .19, [95% CI: .01, .79]), indicating that AAQ-II scores mediated the relationship between PCL-C and ORWELL-97 scores.

Results in the subsample of men only (n = 69) were similar, such that patterns of significance did not differ.

Discussion

In this sample of veterans with overweight/obesity, greater PTSD symptoms were associated with greater binge-eating symptoms and poorer obesity-related quality of life. Experiential avoidance mediated the relationship between PTSD symptoms and obesity-related quality of life, but did not mediate the relationship between PTSD symptoms and binge-eating symptoms.

Our hypothesis that greater PTSD symptoms would be related to greater binge-eating symptoms and lower obesity-related quality of life was supported. These results are consistent with previous findings in male veterans indicating an association between PTSD symptoms and greater endorsement of eating disorder symptoms (Litwack et al., 2014). For example, in a sample of veterans with overweight and obesity, veterans with more clinically meaningful binge-eating behavior were more likely to have a PTSD diagnosis (Higgins et al., 2013). Additionally, in a national sample of civilians, meeting criteria for either PTSD or subthreshold PTSD were more common among both men and women with binge-eating disorder than individuals without binge-eating disorder (Mitchell et al., 2012).

The relationship between PTSD symptoms and worse obesity-related quality of life is also consistent with previous research. Studies have found a relationship between PTSD symptoms and worse health-related quality of life in civilian populations with coronary heart disease (Cohen et al., 2009) and PTSD (Pagotto et al., 2015), as well as veteran populations who are tobacco-dependent (Aversa et al., 2012), and who experienced combat during operation Enduring Freedom/Operation Iraqi Freedom (Pittman et al., 2012). The current study extends these findings to veterans with overweight/obesity and suggests that PTSD symptoms may specifically increase the physical symptoms, discomfort, and impact of obesity.

Our hypothesis that experiential avoidance would mediate the relationship between PTSD symptoms and obesity-related quality of life was supported. Avoidance behaviors among individuals with PTSD are associated with decreased functioning across several domains (Solomon & Mikulincer, 2007), and in one prior study experiential avoidance partially accounted for the relationship between PTSD and quality of life among civilian survivors of the Kosovo war (Kashdan et al., 2009). Kashdan et al. (2009) suggest that PTSD symptoms may contribute to moving away from valued activities, leading to worse quality of life. Our results extend this prior research by showing that experiential avoidance associated with PTSD symptoms among veterans with overweight/obesity may exacerbate the negative impacts of obesity on quality of life. Taken together, treatments targeting experiential avoidance among those with PTSD symptoms may also decrease obesity-related detriments to well-being. Third-wave psychotherapies such as ACT are promising options for those with comorbid PTSD symptoms and obesity-related problems. The ACT model theorizes that experiential avoidance, or the unwillingness to experience unwanted internal events (thoughts, emotions, and physical sensations), is at the root of many psychological and behavioral problems (Hayes et al., 2006). In relation to the present study, mindfulness and acceptance skills around unwanted internal events related to PTSD and weight management could be addressed to encourage adaptive behaviors associated with personal meaning (e.g., accepting feelings of hypervigilance while in public with loved ones in accordance with affiliative values; accepting urges to consume excessive food rather than attempting to avoid them by eating, in according with health values). However, additional research is needed to investigate this hypothesis.

Contrary to predictions, experiential avoidance did not mediate the relationship between PTSD symptoms and binge-eating symptoms. This is surprising given the existing literature suggesting that negative emotions associated with PTSD, such as guilt and anger, tend to precede binge-eating (Dingemans et al., 2017). Previous studies with civilian and primarily female samples that suggest bingeeating functions as means to manage emotions (e.g., Dingemans et al., 2017; Keating et al., 2019) may not generalize to our primarily male veteran sample. For military personnel, bingeeating behaviors may be a means to adapt to the circumstances of military service. For example, veterans may have initially engaged in bingeeating during active duty following the use of compensatory strategies to 'make weight' or because of forming habits around eating quickly in response to situational demands (Masheb et al., 2019). Further, the relationship between PTSD symptoms and engaging in bingeeating may be better explained by alternative processes such as impulsivity, which has also been associated with both PTSD (James et al., 2014; Roley et al., 2017) and bingeeating (Schag et al., 2013). Lastly, only approximately half of our sample met the threshold for clinically meaningful bingeeating symptoms. Therefore, our participants may have less severe deficits in the emotional regulation strategies (e.g., rumination, suppression) that have been identified in samples of participants with binge-eating disorder (Dingemans et al., 2017); however, we did not collect data to assess this. If less severe deficits in these emotional regulation strategies are identified in future work, it would imply emotion regulation is not the ideal target for these individuals, and alternative treatment targets should be identified.

Strengths of the current study include a primarily male veteran sample, which is typically underrepresented in eating disorder research. This study also contributes to the literature by demonstrating one potential mechanism—experiential avoidance—that may explain the relationship between PTSD symptoms and poor obesity-related quality of life among veterans with overweight/obesity. However, these preliminary results must be considered with caution as the study was cross-sectional and cannot be used to draw conclusions related to causality or directionality of relationships. Future research should examine these relationships longitudinally and with a larger sample size to determine directionality of relationships among PTSD symptoms, obesity-related factors, and experiential avoidance. Further, in our sample of veterans with overweight/obesity, participants were not required to meet full criteria for PTSD and/or binge-eating disorder. Consequently, the current study examines broader symptoms of trauma-related and eating disorders. Continued work examining the role of experiential avoidance in samples that meet full diagnostic criteria for BED and/or PTSD is needed to understand and inform treatments for these clinical populations. Data collection commenced before the publication of the Diagnostic and Statistical Manual of Mental Disorders, 5th edition (DSM-5). Therefore, we used the PCL-C to assess PTSD, which was developed based on DSM-IV criteria. Examining relationships between our study variables and DSM-5 diagnostic criteria using updated measures (e.g., the PCL-5) would help identify the role of the added mood and cognitive symptom cluster in explaining the relationships among binge-eating symptoms, experiential avoidance, and PTSD (Weathers et al., 2013). Further, experiential avoidance may play a role in other poor health behaviors associated with both PTSD and obesity, such as physical inactivity (Butryn et al., 2015; Hall et al., 2015). Ultimately, further tailoring and testing of interventions for treating comorbid eating and trauma-related concerns are needed.

The current study is the first to examine experiential avoidance as a potential mechanism explaining the relationship between the broader symptomologies of PTSD and binge-eating and obesity-related quality of life in a sample of veterans with overweight/obesity. The study provides preliminary evidence that experiential avoidance may be an underlying psychological process that explains the relationship between PTSD symptoms and obesity-related quality of life, but not binge-eating symptoms. These cross-sectional results can inform future longitudinal work seeking to identify psychological mechanisms contributing to these commonly co-occurring concerns and the development of targeted treatments to address trauma-related symptoms and binge-eating behaviors simultaneously.

Funding

This project was supported by Veterans Affairs Rehabilitation R&D grant I01RX000381. Drs. Afari and Herbert and Ms. Dochat are partially supported by R01DK106415 from National Institute of Diabetes and Kidney Disease. Dr. Herbert was also supported by VA RR&D CDA Grant 1IK2RX002807-01A2. Dr. Wooldridge is supported by the VA office of academic affiliates advanced fellowship in women's health. The views expressed in this paper are those of the authors and do not reflect the official policy or position on the funding agency, Department of Veterans Affairs, the United States Government, or any institutions with which the authors are affiliated. None of the authors has any conflicts of interest to disclose. Clinicaltrials.gov identifier: NCT03234881

ORCID

Jennalee S. Wooldridge http://orcid.org/0000-0002-2815-5974
Matthew S. Herbert http://orcid.org/0000-0001-7395-6271
Niloofar Afari http://orcid.org/0000-0002-6489-378X

References

Afari, N., Herbert, M. S., Godfrey, K. M., Cuneo, J. G., Salamat, J. S., Mostoufi, S., Gasperi, M., Ober, K., Backhaus, A., Rutledge, T., & Wetherell, J. L. (2019). Acceptance and commitment therapy as an adjunct to the MOVE! programme: A randomized controlled trial. *Obesity Science & Practice*, *5*(5), 397–407. https://doi.org/10.1002/osp4.356

Albano, G., Rowlands, K., Baciadonna, L., Lo Coco, G., & Cardi, V. (2019). Inter personal difficulties in obesity: A systematic review and meta-analysis to inform a rejection sensitivity-based model. *Neuroscience and Biobehavioral Reviews*, *107*, 846–861. https://doi.org/10.1016/j.neubiorev.2019.09.039

Allison, K. C., Grilo, C. M., Masheb, R. M., & Stunkard, A. J. (2005). Binge eating disorder and night eating syndrome: A comparative study of disordered eating. *Journal of Consulting and Clinical Psychology*, *73*(6), 1107–1115. https://doi.org/10.1037/0022-006X.73.6.1107

American Psychiatric Association. (2013). Trauma- and Stressor-Related Disorders. *In Diagnostic and statistical manual of mental disorders* (5th ed.). https://doi.org/10.1176/appi.books.9780890425596.dsm07.

Aversa, L. H., Stoddard, J. A., Doran, N. M., Au, S., Chow, B., McFall, M., Saxon, A., & Baker, D. G. (2012). PTSD and depression as predictors of physical health-related quality of life in tobacco-dependent veterans. *Journal of Psychosomatic Research, 73*(3), 185–190. https://doi.org/10.1016/j.jpsychores.2012.06.010

Barnes, R. D., & Tantleff-Dunn, S. (2010). Food for thought: Examining the relationship between food thought suppression and weight-related outcomes. *Eating Behaviors, 11*(3), 175–179. https://doi.org/10.1016/j.eatbeh.2010.03.001

Bartoli, F., Crocamo, C., Alamia, A., Amidani, F., Paggi, E., Pini, E., Clerici, M., & Carrà, G. (2015). Posttraumatic Stress Disorder and Risk of Obesity. *The Journal of Clinical Psychiatry, 76*(10), e1253–e1261. https://doi.org/10.4088/JCP.14r09199

Bertoli, S., Leone, A., Ponissi, V., Bedogni, G., Beggio, V., Strepparava, M. G., & Battezzati, A. (2016). Prevalence of and risk factors for binge eating behaviour in 6930 adults starting a weight loss or maintenance programme. *Public Health Nutrition, 19*(1), 71–77. https://doi.org/10.1017/S1368980015001068

Biener, A., Cawley, J., & Meyerhoefer, C. (2017). The High and Rising Costs of Obesity to the US Health Care System. *Journal of General Internal Medicine, 32*(S1), 6–8. https://doi.org/10.1007/s11606-016-3968-8

Blanchard, E. B., Jones-Alexander, J., Buckley, T. C., & Forneris, C. A. (1996). Psychometric properties of the PTSD Checklist (PCL). *Behaviour Research and Therapy, 34* (8), 669–673. https://doi.org/10.1016/0005-7967(96)00033-2

Bond, F. W., Hayes, S. C., Baer, R. A., Carpenter, K. M., Guenole, N., Orcutt, H. K., Waltz, T., & Zettle, R. D. (2011). Preliminary Psychometric Properties of the Acceptance and Action Questionnaire–II: A Revised Measure of Psychological Inflexibility and Experiential Avoidance. *Behavior Therapy, 42*(4), 676–688. https://doi.org/10.1016/j.beth.2011.03.007

Breland, J. Y., Phibbs, C. S., Hoggatt, K. J., Washington, D. L., Lee, J., Haskell, S., Uchendu, U. S., Saechao, F. S., Zephyrin, L. C., & Frayne, S. M. (2017). The Obesity Epidemic in the Veterans Health Administration: Prevalence Among Key Populations of Women and Men Veterans. *Journal of General Internal Medicine, 32*(S1), 11–17. https://doi.org/10.1007/s11606-016-3962-1

Brewerton, T. D. (2007). Eating Disorders, Trauma, and Comorbidity: Focus on PTSD. *Eating Disorders, 15*(4), 285–304. https://doi.org/10.1080/10640260701454311

Butryn, M. L., Arigo, D., Raggio, G. A., Kaufman, A. I., Kerrigan, S. G., & Forman, E. M. (2015). Measuring the Ability to Tolerate Activity-Related Discomfort: Initial Validation of the Physical Activity Acceptance Questionnaire (PAAQ). *Journal of Physical Activity & Health, 12*(5), 717–726. https://doi.org/10.1123/jpah.2013-0338

Centers for Disease Control and Prevention (CDC). (2017). *About Adult BMI*. U.S. Department of Health and Human Services. Retrieved July 10, 2019, from https://www.cdc.gov/healthyweight/assessing/bmi/adult_bmi/index.html

Cohen, B. E., Marmar, C. R., Neylan, T. C., Schiller, N. B., Ali, S., & Whooley, M. A. (2009). Posttraumatic stress disorder and health-related quality of life in patients with coronary heart disease: Findings from the heart and soul study. *Archives of General Psychiatry, 66*(11), 1214–1220. https://doi.org/10.1001/archgenpsychiatry.2009.149

De Zwaan, M., Lancaster, K. L., Mitchell, J. E., Howell, L. M., Monson, N., Roerig, J. L., & Crosby, R. D. (2002). Health-related quality of life in morbidly obese patients: Effect of gastric bypass surgery. *Obesity Surgery, 12*(6), 773–780. https://doi.org/10.1381/096089202320995547

Dingemans, A., Danner, U., & Parks, M. (2017, November 22). *Emotion regulation in binge eating disorder: A review. Nutrients*. MDPI AG. https://doi.org/10.3390/nu9111274

Dixon, J. B. (2010). The effect of obesity on health outcomes. *Molecular and Cellular Endocrinology, 316*(2), 104–108. https://doi.org/10.1016/j.mce.2009.07.008

Dorflinger, L. M., Ruser, C. B., & Masheb, R. M. (2017). A brief screening measure for binge eating in primary care. *Eating Behaviors*, *26*, 163–166. https://doi.org/10.1016/j.eatbeh.2017.03.009

Fulton, J. J., Calhoun, P. S., Wagner, H. R., Schry, A. R., Hair, L. P., Feeling, N., Elbogen, E., & Beckham, J. C. (2015, April 1). The prevalence of posttraumatic stress disorder in Operation Enduring Freedom/Operation Iraqi Freedom (OEF/OIF) Veterans: A meta-analysis. *Journal of Anxiety Disorders*, *31*, 98–107. Elsevier Ltd. https://doi.org/10.1016/j.janxdis.2015.02.003

Gormally, J., Black, S., Daston, S., & Rardin, D. (1982). The assessment of binge eating severity among obese persons. *Addictive Behaviors*, *7* (1), 47–55.https://doi.org/10.1016/0306-4603(82)90024-7

Greeno, C. G., Marcus, M. D., & Wing, R. R. (1995). Diagnosis of binge eating disorder: Discrepancies between a questionnaire and clinical interview. *International Journal of Eating Disorders*, *17*(2), 153–160. https://doi.org/10.1002/1098-108X(199503)17:2<153::AID-EAT2260170208>3.0.CO;2-V

Hall, K. S., Hoerster, K. D., & Yancy, W. S. (2015). Post-Traumatic Stress Disorder, Physical Activity, and Eating Behaviors. *Epidemiologic Reviews*, *37*(1), 103–115. https://doi.org/10.1093/epirev/mxu011

Hayes, S. C., Luoma, J. B., Bond, F. W., Masuda, A., & Lillis, J. (2006). Acceptance and Commitment Therapy: Model, processes and outcomes. *Behaviour Research and Therapy*, *44*(1), 1–25. https://doi.org/10.1016/j.brat.2005.06.006

Higgins, D. M., Dorflinger, L., MacGregor, K. L., Heapy, A. A., Goulet, J. L., & Ruser, C. (2013). Binge eating behavior among a national sample of overweight and obese veterans. *Obesity*, *21*(5), 900–903. https://doi.org/10.1002/oby.20160

Holzer, S. R., Uppala, S., Wonderlich, S. A., Crosby, R. D., & Simonich, H. (2008). Mediational significance of PTSD in the relationship of sexual trauma and eating disorders. *Child Abuse & Neglect*, *32*(5), 561–566. https://doi.org/10.1016/j.chiabu.2007.07.011

James, L. M., Strom, T. Q., & Leskela, J. (2014). Risk-taking behaviors and impulsivity among veterans with and without PTSD and mild TBI. *Military Medicine*, *179*(4), 357–363. https://doi.org/10.7205/MILMED-D-13-00241

Jensen, M. (2016). Obesity. In L. Goldman & A. Schafer (Eds.), *Goldman-Cecil Medicine* (25th ed.). Elsevier Saunders, 1409–1417.

Jia, H., & Lubetkin, E. I. (2005). The impact of obesity on health-related quality-of-life in the general adult US population. *Journal of Public Health*, *27*(2), 156–164. https://doi.org/10.1093/pubmed/fdi025

Kang, H. K. (2003). Post-traumatic stress disorder and chronic fatigue syndrome-like illness among gulf war veterans: A population-based survey of 30,000 veterans. *American Journal of Epidemiology*, *157*(2), 141–148. https://doi.org/10.1093/aje/kwf187

Kashdan, T. B., Morina, N., & Priebe, S. (2009). Post-traumatic stress disorder, social anxiety disorder, and depression in survivors of the Kosovo War: Experiential avoidance as a contributor to distress and quality of life. *Journal of Anxiety Disorders*, *23*(2), 185–196. https://doi.org/10.1016/j.janxdis.2008.06.006

Keating, L., Mills, J. S., & Rawana, J. S. (2019). Momentary predictors of binge eating: An attachment perspective. *Eating Behaviors*, *32*, 44–52. https://doi.org/10.1016/j.eatbeh.2018.12.003

Lecrubier, Y., Sheehan, D. V., Weiller, E., Amorim, P., Bonora, I., Sheehan, K. H., Janavs, J., & Dunbar, G. C. (1997). The Mini International Neuropsychiatric Interview (MINI). A short diagnostic structured interview: Reliability and validity according to the CIDI. *European Psychiatry*, *12*(5), 224–231. https://doi.org/10.1016/S0924-9338(97)83296-8

Lillis, J., Hayes, S. C., Bunting, K., & Masuda, A. (2009). Teaching Acceptance and Mindfulness to Improve the Lives of the Obese: A Preliminary Test of a Theoretical Model. *Annals of Behavioral Medicine*, *37*(1), 58–69. https://doi.org/10.1007/s12160-009-9083-x

Lillis, J., Hayes, S. C., & Levin, M. E. (2011). Binge eating and weight control: The role of experiential avoidance. *Behavior Modification*, *35*(3), 252–264. https://doi.org/10.1177/0145445510397178

Lillis, J., Levin, M. E., & Hayes, S. C. (2011). Exploring the relationship between body mass index and health-related quality of life: A pilot study of the impact of weight self-stigma and experiential avoidance. *Journal of Health Psychology*, *16*(5), 722–727. https://doi.org/10.1177/1359105310388321

Litwack, S. D., Mitchell, K. S., Sloan, D. M., Reardon, A. F., & Miller, M. W. (2014). Eating disorder symptoms and comorbid psychopathology among male and female veterans. *General Hospital Psychiatry*, *36*(4), 406–410. https://doi.org/10.1016/j.genhosppsych.2014.03.013

Mannucci, E., Ricca, V., Barciulli, E., Di Bernardo, M., Travaglini, R., Cabras, P. L., & Rotella, C. M. (1999). Quality of life and overweight: The obesity related well-being (Orwell 97) questionnaire. *Addictive Behaviors*, *24* (3), 345–357. https://doi.org/10.1016/S0306-4603(98)00055-0.

Marmar, C. R., Schlenger, W., Henn-Haase, C., Qian, M., Purchia, E., Li, M., Corry, N., Williams, C. S., Ho, C.-L., Horesh, D., Karstoft, K.-I., Shalev, A., & Kulka, R. A. (2015). Course of posttraumatic stress disorder 40 years after the Vietnam war findings from the national Vietnam veterans longitudinal study. *JAMA Psychiatry*, *72*(9), 875–881. https://doi.org/10.1001/jamapsychiatry.2015.0803

Masheb, R. M., Kutz, A. M., Marsh, A. G., Min, K. M., Ruser, C. B., & Dorflinger, L. M. (2019). "Making weight" during military service is related to binge eating and eating pathology for veterans later in life. *Eating and Weight Disorders - Studies on Anorexia, Bulimia and Obesity*, *24*(6), 1063–1070. https://doi.org/10.1007/s40519-019-00766-w

Masheb, R. M., Lutes, L. D., Myra Kim, H., Holleman, R. G., Goodrich, D. E., Janney, C. A., Kirsh, S., Richardson, C. R., & Damschroder, L. J. (2015). High-frequency binge eating predicts weight gain among veterans receiving behavioral weight loss treatments. *Obesity*, *23* (1), 54–61. https://doi.org/10.1002/oby.20931

Mason, S. M., Frazier, P. A., Austin, S. B., Harlow, B. L., Jackson, B., Raymond, N. C., & Rich-Edwards, J. W. (2017). Posttraumatic Stress Disorder Symptoms and Problematic Overeating Behaviors in Young Men and Women. *Annals of Behavioral Medicine*, *51*(6), 822–832. https://doi.org/10.1007/s12160-017-9905-1

Mitchell, K. S., Mazzeo, S. E., Schlesinger, M. R., Brewerton, T. D., & Smith, B. N. (2012, April). Comorbidity of partial and subthreshold PTSD among men and women with eating disorders in the national comorbidity survey-replication study. *International Journal of Eating Disorders*, *45*(3), 307–315. https://doi.org/10.1002/eat.20965

Pagotto, L. F., Mendlowicz, M. V., Coutinho, E. S. F., Figueira, I., Luz, M. P., Araujo, A. X., & Berger, W. (2015). The impact of posttraumatic symptoms and comorbid mental disorders on the health-related quality of life in treatment-seeking PTSD patients. *Comprehensive Psychiatry*, *58*, 68–73. https://doi.org/10.1016/j.comppsych.2015.01.002

Pittman, J. O. E., Goldsmith, A. A., Lemmer, J. A., Kilmer, M. T., & Baker, D. G. (2012). Posttraumatic stress disorder, depression, and health-related quality of life in OEF/OIF veterans. *Quality of Life Research*, *21*(1), 99–103. https://doi.org/10.1007/s11136-011-9918-3

Preacher, K. J., & Hayes, A. F. (2004). SPSS and SAS procedures for estimating indirect effects in simple mediation models. *Behavior Research Methods, Instruments and Computers*, *36*(4), 717–731. https://doi.org/10.3758/BF03206553

Roley, M. E., Contractor, A. A., Weiss, N. H., Armour, C., & Elhai, J. D. (2017). Impulsivity facets' predictive relations with DSM-5 PTSD symptom clusters. *Psychological Trauma: Theory, Research, Practice, and Policy*, *9*(1), 76–79. https://doi.org/10.1037/tra0000146

Rosenberger, P. H., & Dorflinger, L. (2013). Psychosocial factors associated with binge eating among overweight and obese male veterans. *Eating Behaviors*, *14*(3), 401–404. https://doi.org/10.1016/j.eatbeh.2013.06.006

Schag, K., Schönleber, J., Teufel, M., Zipfel, S., & Giel, K. E. (2013). Food-related impulsivity in obesity and Binge Eating Disorder - a systematic review. *Obesity Reviews*, *14*(6), 477–495. https://doi.org/10.1111/obr.12017

Scott, K. M., McGee, M. A., Wells, J. E., & Oakley Browne, M. A. (2008). Obesity and mental disorders in the adult general population. *Journal of Psychosomatic Research*, *64*(1), 97–105. https://doi.org/10.1016/j.jpsychores.2007.09.006

Short, N. A., Boffa, J. W., Clancy, K., & Schmidt, N. B. (2018). Effects of emotion regulation strategy use in response to stressors on PTSD symptoms: An ecological momentary assessment study. *Journal of Affective Disorders*, *230*, 77–83. https://doi.org/10.1016/j.jad.2017.12.063

Slane, J. D., Levine, M. D., Borrero, S., Mattocks, K. M., Ozier, A. D., Silliker, N., Bathulapalli, H., Brandt, C., & Haskell, S. G. (2016). Eating behaviors: Prevalence, psychiatric comorbidity, and associations with body mass index among male and female Iraq and Afghanistan Veterans. *Military Medicine*, *181*(11), e1650–e1656. https://doi.org/10.7205/MILMED-D-15-00482

Smith, B. N., Tyzik, A. L., Neylan, T. C., & Cohen, B. E. (2015). PTSD and obesity in younger and older veterans: Results from the mind your heart study. *Psychiatry Research*, *229*(3), 895–900. https://doi.org/10.1016/j.psychres.2015.07.044

Solomon, Z., & Mikulincer, M. (2007). Posttraumatic intrusion, avoidance, and social functioning: A 20-year longitudinal study. *Journal of Consulting and Clinical Psychology*, *75*(2), 316–324. https://doi.org/10.1037/0022-006X.75.2.316

Talbot, L. S., Maguen, S., Epel, E. S., Metzler, T. J., & Neylan, T. C. (2013). Posttraumatic stress disorder is associated with emotional eating. *Journal of Traumatic Stress*, *26*(4), 521–525. https://doi.org/10.1002/jts.21824

Tapper, K., Shaw, C., Ilsley, J., Hill, A. J., Bond, F. W., & Moore, L. (2009). Exploratory randomised controlled trial of a mindfulness-based weight loss intervention for women. *Appetite*, *52*(2), 396–404. https://doi.org/10.1016/j.appet.2008.11.012

Valente, S., Di Girolamo, G., Forlani, M., Biondini, A., Scudellari, P., De Ronchi, D., & Atti, A. R. (2017). Sex-specific issues in eating disorders: A clinical and psychopathological investigation. *Eating and Weight Disorders*, *22*(4), 707–715. https://doi.org/10.1007/s40519-017-0432-7

Vieweg, W. V. R., Julius, D. A., Bates, J., Quinn, J. F., Fernandez, A., Hasnain, M., & Pandurangi, A. K. (2007). Posttraumatic stress disorder as a risk factor for obesity among male military veterans. *Acta psychiatrica Scandinavica*, *116*(6), 483–487. https://doi.org/10.1111/j.1600-0447.2007.01071.x

Weathers, F., Litz, B., Keane, T. M., Palmieri, P. A., Marx, B. P., & Schnurr, P. P. (2013, August). The PTSD Checklist for DSM-5 (PCL-5). *National Center for PTSD*, *5*, 2002. https://doi.org/10.1037/t02622-000

Weineland, S., Lillis, J., & Dahl, J. (2013). Measuring experiential avoidance in a bariatric surgery population—Psychometric properties of AAQ-W. *Obesity Research & Clinical Practice*, *7*(6), e464–e475. https://doi.org/10.1016/j.orcp.2012.06.002

Examining the roles of emotion dysregulation and impulsivity in the relationship between psychological trauma and substance abuse among women with bulimic-spectrum pathology

Lauren M. Schaefer, Vivienne M. Hazzard, Kathryn E. Smith, Cassandra A. Johnson, Li Cao, Ross D. Crosby, Carol B. Peterson, Scott J. Crow, Anna M. Bardone-Cone, Thomas E. Joiner, Daniel Le Grange, Marjorie H. Klein, James E. Mitchell, and Stephen A. Wonderlich

ABSTRACT

Individuals with bulimia nervosa report elevated rates of childhood maltreatment, which appears to increase risk for co-occurring substance use problems and negatively impact clinical course. The current study sought to examine the mechanistic pathways by which specific forms of childhood maltreatment may give rise to substance use problems among individuals with bulimic-spectrum pathology. Women with bulimic-spectrum disorders ($N = 204$) completed measures of childhood trauma, emotion dysregulation, impulsivity, and substance use. Path analysis was used to examine emotion dysregulation and impulsivity as mediators of the relationship between distinct forms of childhood trauma (physical abuse, physical neglect, emotional abuse, emotional neglect, and sexual abuse) and the presence of problematic alcohol/drug use. In the full path model, significant pathways from childhood emotional abuse to emotion dysregulation, childhood emotional neglect to impulsivity, and emotion dysregulation to problematic substance use emerged. Further, emotion dysregulation significantly mediated the relationship between emotional abuse and substance use. Results indicate that emotion dysregulation may be an important mechanism linking a history of childhood emotional maltreatment to later eating and substance use problems, and therefore may be an important treatment target among individuals with co-occurring eating and substance use concerns.

- Childhood emotional abuse was related to greater emotion dysregulation.

- Childhood emotional neglect was related to greater impulsivity.
- Emotion dysregulation was related to greater problematic substance use.
- Emotional abuse may impact substance use through emotion dysregulation.
- Creating emotion dysregulation may improve substance and eating disorder symptoms.

A large body of research indicates that eating disorders (ED) and substance use disorders (SUD) are highly comorbid. For example, the National Center on Addiction and Substance Abuse (CASA) at Columbia University (2003) estimates that roughly 50% of women with an ED engage in abuse of substances, and recent meta-analytic evidence suggests that one in five individuals with an ED will develop an SUD during their lifetime (Bahji et al., 2019). In particular, bulimic-spectrum disorders, such as bulimia nervosa (BN), which are characterized by recurrent binge eating (i.e., overeating accompanied by a sense of having lost control) and purging (e.g., self-induced vomiting, laxative abuse to prevent weight gain), are marked by especially high rates of co-occurring substance use problems compared to disorders primarily characterized by dietary restriction (Bahji et al., 2019; Baker et al., 2010). Importantly, comorbid substance use problems among individuals with EDs significantly compound psychological impairments, and negatively impact clinical course and outcomes (Gregorowski et al., 2013; Harrop & Marlatt, 2010), highlighting the importance of interventions targeting common etiological and maintenance factors (Dennis & Pryor, 2018; Dennis et al., 2014). Towards this end, clarification of factors that contribute to substance use among individuals with bulimic-spectrum disorders may help to inform prevention and treatment approaches for this population.

Psychological trauma, particularly when experienced in childhood, has been identified as a risk factor for a broad range of psychological disorders including EDs and SUDs. For example, research indicates that individuals with eating pathology report elevated rates of childhood maltreatment (i.e., abuse and neglect) (Caslini et al., 2016; Molendijk et al., 2017; Smolak & Murnen, 2002), and that a history of childhood maltreatment increases risk for later substance use problems (Enoch, 2011). While some research has examined the association between childhood maltreatment broadly defined (i.e., assessed as a single unitary construct) and overall eating pathology, other studies have attempted to parse apart relationships between specific adverse childhood experiences and specific ED behaviors. A meta-analytic review of this literature demonstrates elevated levels of sexual, physical, and emotional maltreatment among individuals with BN compared to healthy controls, and indicates a stronger association between BN and experiences of childhood emotional maltreatment compared to other forms of abuse (Molendijk et al., 2017). Similarly, emotional abuse and neglect have been identified as key risk factors for substance use problems (Moustafa et al., 2021), suggesting that emotional maltreatment may be a particularly powerful risk factor for both eating and substance use disorders.

Recognition of the detrimental impact of childhood maltreatment on psychological outcomes in adulthood has motivated theoretical and empirical work examining the mechanisms by which traumatic early life experiences lead to enduring emotional and behavioral dysfunction. In particular, abusive or neglectful interpersonal experiences during this key developmental period may contribute to difficulties regulating emotions (e.g., understanding, tolerating, and adaptively coping with emotional distress) and greater impulsivity (e.g., a tendency towards engaging in rash actions or decision-making, difficulty sustaining attention) (Trottier & MacDonald, 2017), which then elevate risk for more severe psychiatric illness. For example, growing up in an environment characterized by high levels of criticism or punishment of emotional expression and/or minimization of emotional experiences, which are typical of emotional abuse, may contribute to emotion regulation deficits such as emotional suppression and avoidant coping (Burns et al., 2012). In turn, individuals may utilize maladaptive means (e.g., binge eating or substance use) to suppress or escape from unwanted emotional experiences (Heatherton & Baumeister, 1991). In an alternative, or perhaps complementary process, parents who are themselves prone to rash or impulsive actions may be more likely to engage in abuse or neglect of others, which may contribute to impulsivity in abused or neglected children via modeling, disrupted neural development, and/or hereditary processes (Liu, 2019). This impulsivity may then contribute to the development of specific forms of psychopathology characterized by repeated engagement in rash, harmful, or short-term-oriented behavior (e.g., substance misuse, binge eating, purging), which may also serve to reduce unpleasant affective experiences.

Consistent with these hypotheses, research examining the downstream effects of childhood maltreatment suggests a strong association between early experiences of abuse, especially emotional abuse, and later problems with impulsivity (Liu, 2019) and emotion dysregulation (Cloitre et al., 2005; Pollak, 2008). Further, deficits in emotion regulation and impulse control are consistently observed among individuals with EDs (Lavender et al., 2015; Smith et al., 2018) and SUDs (Lee et al., 2019; Sloan et al., 2017). Studies using mediational approaches provide additional support for the hypothesized relations, indicating that emotion dysregulation and impulsivity each mediate the association between childhood maltreatment and ED symptoms (Burns et al., 2012; Dworkin et al., 2014; Moulton et al., 2015), as well as between childhood maltreatment and substance use problems (Oshri et al., 2018; Weiss et al., 2019).

Limited research has examined relationships between distinct forms of childhood maltreatment, emotion dysregulation, impulsivity, and substance abuse among individuals with BN symptomatology. However, such work may help to clarify the mechanisms through which early abuse experiences contribute to comorbid substance use problems within this population. As evidence suggests that specific forms of childhood trauma may exhibit differential relationships with problematic outcomes, it is possible that different types of maltreatment may lead to the combination of EDs and substance abuse use via different mechanistic pathways.

In order to investigate this possibility, the current study sought to examine the relationship between childhood trauma and comorbid substance use among individuals with bulimic-spectrum pathology. Specifically, path analysis was used to examine emotion dysregulation and impulsivity as mediators of the relationship between distinct forms of childhood trauma (i.e., physical abuse, physical neglect, emotional abuse, emotional neglect, and sexual abuse) and the presence of comorbid problematic alcohol/drug use. Consistent with previous findings among individuals with SUDS (Oshri et al., 2018; Weiss et al., 2019), we expected emotion dysregulation and impulsivity to mediate the associations between childhood maltreatment and substance use problems in this sample of individuals with bulimic-spectrum pathology. In light of existing research demonstrating the relative importance of emotional forms of maltreatment in the development of SUDs and problems of emotion and impulse regulation (Cloitre et al., 2005; Liu, 2019; Moustafa et al., 2021; Pollak, 2008), we further hypothesized that emotional abuse and neglect would evidence the strongest associations with examined downstream outcomes.

Methods

Participants

The present study represents a secondary analysis of cross-sectional data that were originally collected to examine correlates of bulimic-spectrum disorders (for examples of additional studies utilizing this dataset see; Anestis et al., 2009; Bardone-Cone et al., 2008; Brownstone et al., 2013; Wonderlich et al., 2005). The sample included 204 women with bulimic-spectrum pathology recruited from five sites in the midwestern United States (Chicago, IL; Columbia, MO; Fargo, ND; Madison, WI; Minneapolis, MN). The study was promoted via advertisements in eating disorder clinics and the surrounding communities. To be eligible for the study, participants were required to be between the ages of 18–65, female gender, and engaging in regular binge eating and purging behavior. Exclusion criteria for the study included active psychotic symptoms, neurocognitive disorders, and the inability to read or understand English. Based on a telephone interview, 144 women (71%) met full diagnostic criteria for BN according to the Diagnostic and Statistical Manual of Mental Disorders, 4th edition (DSM-IV; American Psychiatric Association, 1994), and 60 women (29%) met criteria for subthreshold BN, defined as (a) objective binge eating and compensatory behavior occurring at least once per week over the past 3 months, or (b) compensatory behavior occurring at least once per week along with subjective binge eating. The majority of participants were single or never married (74.9%), Caucasian (90.7%), and had received some education beyond high school (93.1%). Participants ranged in age from 18 to 57 years old ($M = 25.7$, $SD = 8.8$ years), with an average BMI of 22.9 kg/m^2 ($SD = 5.2$). Although the DSM-5 does not provide a universal cutoff for defining "significantly low weight," 21 participants (10% of the sample) had a BMI of 18.5 or less, which is considered to be underweight according to the Centers for Disease Control and Prevention (Centers for Disease Control and Prevention, 2020) and World Health Organization (World Health Organization, 2020).

Procedure

Trained interviewers administered a brief diagnostic telephone interview that included the eating disorder module of the Structured Clinical Interview for DSM-IV, Patient Edition (SCID-P) to assess eligibility. Eligible individuals were invited to participate in the study and scheduled for an in-person appointment during which they provided informed consent and completed self-report measures. Participants were compensated 50 USD for their time. The study protocol was reviewed and approved by the Institutional Review Boards at each of the recruiting sites.

Measures

The structured clinical interview for DSM-IV, patient edition (SCID-P)

The SCID-P eating disorder module (First et al., 1995) was administered during the telephone screen to determine diagnostic eligibility. The SCID-P has demonstrated excellent reliability for diagnosing BN in previous studies (Crosby et al., 2009).

Short form of the childhood trauma questionnaire (CTQ-SF)

The CTQ-SF (Bernstein et al., 2003) is a 28-item self-report measure of abuse and neglect experienced during childhood. Respondents indicate the frequency of specific traumatic experiences on a Likert-type scale, with selections ranging from 0 (*never*) to 5 (*very often*). The CTQ-SF comprises five subscales

(Physical Abuse, Sexual Abuse, Emotional Abuse, Emotional Neglect, and Physical Neglect), with higher subscale scores indicating greater levels of abuse. CTQ-SF scores have demonstrated good reliability and validity in prior research (Bernstein et al., 2003; Spinhoven et al., 2014). In the current sample, Cronbach's alpha for the CTQ-SF subscales was 0.58 for Physical Neglect, 0.69 for Physical Abuse, 0.83 for Emotional Abuse, 0.85 for Emotional Neglect, and 0.94 for Sexual Abuse.

Dimensional assessment of personality pathology–basic questionnaire (DAPP-BQ)

The DAPP-BQ (Livesley et al., 1992) is a 290-item self-report questionnaire comprised 18 subscales, which contribute to four weighted higher-order factors (Livesley et al., 1998). The current investigation utilized the Emotional Dysregulation higher-order factor score, which reflects unstable affective responding and interpersonal problems. Respondents rate each statement on a Likert scale ranging from 1 (*strongly disagree*) to 5 (*strongly agree*), with higher factor scores indicating greater emotion dysregulation. The DAPP-BQ has demonstrated good psychometric properties in prior studies (Livesley & Jackson, 2009). Due to the weighted scoring of these higher-order factors, it is not appropriate to calculate Cronbach's alphas.

Barratt impulsiveness scale, version 11 (BIS-11)

The BIS-11 (Barratt, 1959; Patton et al., 1995) is a 30-item self-report questionnaire assessing the personality and behavioral dimensions of impulsiveness. The measure comprises three impulsivity subscales (Motor, Attentional, and Nonplanning) that contribute to a total score in which higher scores indicate greater levels of impulsivity. Participants indicate the frequency of impulsive thoughts and actions on a Likert-type scale, with selections ranging from 1 (*rarely/never*) to 4 (*almost always*). BIS-11 scores have demonstrated good internal consistency and validity in previous studies (Steiger et al., 2001). In the current study, Cronbach's alpha for BIS-11 total score was .85.

Michigan assessment screening test/alcohol-drug (MAST/AD)

The MAST/AD (Westermeyer et al., 2009) is a 25-item self-report questionnaire that assesses the severity of alcohol and drug problems. Respondents indicate the presence/absence of drug and alcohol-related concerns on a dichotomous yes/no scale, with higher weighted total scores signifying greater substance use problems. The MAST/AD has demonstrated good psychometric properties in previous research (Westermeyer et al., 2009). In the present study, the Kuder-Richardson KR-20 coefficient for the MAST/AD was .76. In order to examine statistical predictors of problematic or clinically-meaningful levels of substance use a cutoff of 5 was used to identify individuals with harmful or hazardous substance use, which is consistent with recommendations (Dawe & Mattick, 1997; Selzer, 1971).

Statistical analysis

Missing data for each variable in the path model were low at 1% or less. Further, data were missing completely at random (MCAR) based on Little's MCAR test, $\chi^2(3) = 6.46$, $p = .09$. Therefore, missing data were not imputed. Means, standard deviations, and intercorrelations for all scales were calculated. Next, the full hypothesized model was examined using path analysis with full information maximum likelihood estimation in Mplus version 8.1. As the dependent variable (i.e., MAST/AD scores) was modelled as a dichotomous variable (using the recommended cutoff of 5 for hazardous substance use), logistic regression was employed, precluding an examination of absolute fit indices. Indirect effects were tested using a bias-corrected bootstrapping method. Estimates of indirect effects were evaluated using bootstrapped confidence intervals based on 1,000 resamples. Indirect effects are considered statistically significant when the 95% confidence interval does not include zero. Standardized regression coefficients for all direct and indirect effects are presented for ease of interpretation and comparison of effects.

Results

Means, standard deviations, and intercorrelations among variables are presented in Table 1. Sixty-four percent of the sample ($n = 129$) reported problematic substance use. The hypothesized model accounted for 12% of the variance in emotion dysregulation scores (small to medium effect; Cohen, 1988), 8% of the variance in impulsivity scores (small effect; Cohen, 1988), and six percent of the variance in substance use scores (small effect; Cohen, 1988). Figure 1 presents the standardized path coefficients for the full model. In the full path model, there was a significant pathway from childhood emotional abuse to emotion dysregulation, and from childhood emotional neglect to impulsivity; however, only the pathway from emotion dysregulation to

Table 1. Means, standard deviations, and intercorrelations among study variables (N = 204).

	Mean (SD)	1	2	3	4	5	6	7
1. Sexual Abuse	7.27 (4.72)	—						
2. Emotional Abuse	11.00 (5.50)	.44***	–					
3. Physical Abuse	6.92 (3.29)	.58***	.55***	–				
4. Emotional Neglect	11.29 (5.56)	.35***	.76***	.52***	–			
5. Physical Neglect	7.21 (3.40)	.30***	.60***	.52***	.68***	–		
6. Emotion Dysregulation	51.29 (13.41)	.04	.30***	.07	.30***	.18**	–	
7. Impulsivity	71.25 (11.46)	.01	.16*	.11	.25***	.24**	.36***	–
8. Substance Use	9.28 (10.47)	.07	.09	.15*	.08	.16*	.09	.16*

Note. Sexual Abuse, Emotional Abuse, Physical Abuse, Emotional Neglect, Physical Neglect = all subscales from the Childhood Trauma Questionnaire; Impulsivity = Barratt Impulsiveness Scale; Emotion Dysregulation = Dimensional Assessment of Personality Pathology—Basic Questionnaire-Emotional Dysregulation Factor; Substance Use = Michigan Assessment Screening Test/Alcohol-Drug.

* $p < .05$.

** $p < .01$.

*** $p < .001$.

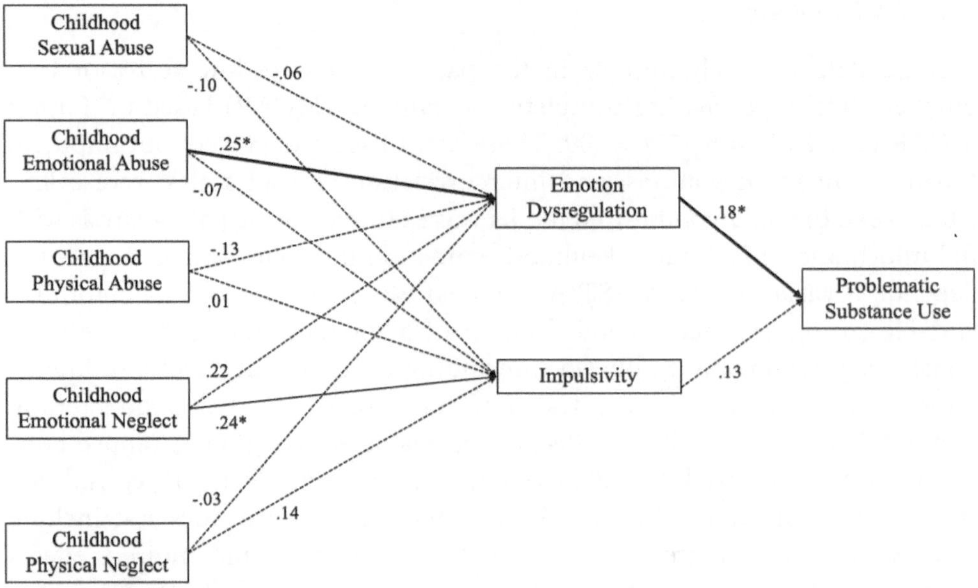

Figure 1. Standardized regression coefficients from path analysis of the full model. Solid lines indicate significant pathways, dashed lines indicate non-significant pathways. Bolded lines indicate significant indirect pathways identified in the post-hoc path analysis. $^{*}p < .05$.

problematic substance use was significant. None of the indirect effects were significant within the full path model. However, the CTQ subscales were strongly intercorrelated, and scores on the BIS-11 and DAPP-BQ Emotion Dysregulation subscale were moderately correlated, which may have obscured individual effects. Although multicollinearity appeared to be low (variance inflation factors all <3.0), we chose to probe for a possible indirect effect of childhood emotional abuse on problematic substance abuse via emotion dysregulation, given the observed direct effects between these variables. To do this, we conducted a post-hoc path analysis, in which childhood emotional abuse was specified as the single independent variable, emotion dysregulation was specified as the single mediator, and problematic substance use was identified as the final dependent variable. This analysis revealed an indirect effect of emotional abuse on substance use via emotion dysregulation (total indirect effect = .07; 95% CI: .01, .15).

Discussion

The current study sought to test a model of comorbid substance use among individuals with bulimic-spectrum pathology, in which distinct forms of childhood maltreatment were expected to contribute to problematic substance use via deficits in emotion regulation and impulse control. Results from the path analytic test of this model indicated an indirect effect of childhood emotional abuse on substance use problems via emotion dysregulation. Although the direct pathway from childhood emotional neglect to impulsivity in adulthood was significant, the path from impulsivity to comorbid substance abuse was not. Thus, results suggest that emotion dysregulation may serve as a particularly important mechanism linking a history of childhood emotional trauma to co-occurring substance abuse in this population.

The high prevalence of problematic substance use observed in the present study aligns with previous research finding high rates of comorbidity between bulimic-spectrum disorders and SUDs (Bahji et al., 2019) and further emphasizes the need to identify shared risk and maintenance factors for these frequently co-occurring disorders. Consistent with prior research indicating an association between emotional abuse and emotion dysregulation (Soenke et al., 2010), the present study also provides support for the unique contribution of childhood emotional abuse in the later development of emotion dysregulation. That is, children who experience frequent verbal attacks on their sense of well-being or self-worth, and/or whose emotional experiences are minimized, criticized, or punished, may later struggle to identify, tolerate, and regulate their own emotional experiences in adulthood as a result. Further, the observed link between emotion dysregulation and problematic substance use within the current sample of women with bulimic-spectrum pathology is consistent with growing evidence supporting emotion dysregulation as a broad transdiagnostic risk factor leading to multiple forms of psychopathology (Sloan et al., 2017). One possible explanation for this finding is that individuals who experience strong emotional reactivity, which they are not equipped to adaptively manage, may seek out alternative and less adaptive means of altering or escaping from aversive emotional states through binge eating or heavy substance use (Heatherton & Baumeister, 1991). Finally, the indirect effect of childhood emotional abuse on problematic substance use via emotion dysregulation coheres with several studies finding specific indirect effects of childhood emotional abuse on ED symptoms through emotion dysregulation in community samples (Burns et al., 2012; Mills et al., 2015; Moulton et al., 2015). The present study extends research in this area by identifying a similar mechanism for substance use problems in a sample of women with bulimic-spectrum disorders, thereby bolstering the evidence that emotion dysregulation plays an important role in the pathway from emotional abuse to psychopathology in this group.

Similarly, impulsivity demonstrated a unique association with emotional neglect in the present study, which is consistent with prior research indicating a robust relationship between emotional forms of childhood maltreatment and difficulties with impulse control (Liu, 2019). It is possible that children whose basic psychological and emotional needs (e.g., love, belonging, support) are neglected may go on to develop a more self-neglectful (or less self-protective) style, potentially giving rise to greater engagement in risk-taking behaviors.

Although impulsivity demonstrated a small bivariate association with substance use, the pathway from impulsivity to problematic substance use was not significant in the final path model. This finding is in contrast with previous literature suggesting that impulsivity is a core etiological factor in substance use (Lee et al., 2019). Notably, impulsivity has been conceptualized as a multidimensional construct comprised several distinct facets (e.g., sensation seeking, lack of planning, lack of perseverance, positive urgency, and negative urgency; Whiteside & Lynam, 2001), which may be differentially related to eating pathology and substance use problems (Dick et al., 2010; Lavender & Mitchell, 2015). While the current study assessed both cognitive and behavioral elements of impulsivity via the Barratt Impulsiveness Scale, it is possible that our use of a broad measure of impulsivity may have obscured more nuanced relationships between substance use problems and individual elements of impulsivity. In addition, the current study assessed impulsivity using a subjective self-report measure, which may be more susceptible to bias than other assessment methods (e.g., interview, behavioral task). Finally, substance use problems were modeled as a dichotomous variable in the path analysis to examine the presence or absence of pathological levels of substance use, which was deemed to be of greatest clinical relevance. Given the bivariate association between BIS-11 and MAST/AD scores, impulsivity may relate to higher but not necessarily pathological levels of substance use among individuals with bulimic-spectrum disorders.

The current study has a number of notable strengths including the use of a semi-structured clinical interview to establish the presence of BN symptoms and the use of validated measures to assess trauma and hypothesized outcomes of interest. However, limitations of the current study must also be noted. As the sample was selected to comprise only females with bulimic-spectrum pathology and the majority of participants were Caucasian and relatively well-educated, results may not generalize to the larger population of individuals with BN symptomatology. Therefore, studies employing more diverse samples are warranted. Further, consistent with transdiagnostic approaches to eating disorders, the sample was specifically recruited to include individuals reporting regular binge eating and purging behavior, characteristic of bulimic-spectrum pathology. Notably, a number of participants (10% of the sample) reported being significantly underweight (according to CDC and WHO guidelines) at the time of the assessment and/or experiencing subjective binge-eating episodes, suggesting that a diagnosis of anorexia binge-eating/purging (AN-BP) type may best describe a portion of the sample. As prior research suggests that the function underlying binge/purge behaviors may differ across AN-BP and BN diagnoses (Elran-Barak et al., 2015), further research should seek to clarify the relationships between examined variables within distinct diagnostic groups. In addition, although types of childhood maltreatment often co-occur (Kim et al., 2017) and moderate to strong correlations were observed between maltreatment types in the present study, individual maltreatment types were examined separately (i.e., with a variable-centered approach rather than with a person-centered approach taking the full maltreatment profile into account). Although this approach represents a strength in that prior research has frequently explored childhood maltreatment as a whole or examined only select forms of maltreatment (e.g., sexual abuse) in isolation, additional research examining individual trauma profiles indicating different types of maltreatment will be informative. For example, empirical classification approaches, such as latent profile analysis, may provide valuable information regarding the specific combinations of childhood abuse that confer greatest risk. Furthermore, the internal consistency for CTQ subscales assessing physical abuse and neglect were suboptimal, which is consistent with prior work demonstrating lower Cronbach's alpha among these scales (Bernstein & Fink, 1998). Therefore, results pertaining to these subscales should be interpreted with caution. In addition, the present study assessed problematic substance use with a self-report questionnaire, and future investigations may seek to examine associations with SUD diagnoses confirmed by clinical interview. Finally, although the current study assessed childhood maltreatment experiences as a child and a teenager, and all other assessments captured current levels of disturbance in adulthood, the cross-sectional nature of the study precludes conclusions regarding temporality and causality. Future longitudinal research is necessary to investigate the effect of adverse childhood experiences on subsequent psychopathology amongst this population.

With regard to clinical implications, the finding that emotional forms of childhood maltreatment may be closely related to broad emotional and behavioral disturbances in adulthood underscores the need for early intervention efforts to address the psychological sequalae of these frequently overlooked forms of abuse. In particular, as emotion dysregulation appeared to operate as a key mechanism linking emotional abuse to substance abuse among women with bulimic-spectrum pathology, emphasizing emotion regulation skills among individuals who have experienced childhood maltreatment may help to protect against the development of subsequent behavioral and psychological disturbances. Further, use of interventions, which address emotion dysregulation among individuals with co-occurring eating and substance abuse problems may be particularly fruitful. For example, Integrative Cognitive-Affective Therapy (ICAT; Wonderlich et al., 2015), which targets emotion dysregulation (Peterson et al., 2017), has demonstrated efficacy among individuals with BN, and particularly those with elevated levels of affective lability (Accurso et al., 2016). Similarly, dialectical behavior therapy (DBT; Linehan, 1993, 2015), which teaches skills for identifying and regulating emotions, appears to be beneficial among individuals with EDs, SUDs, and trauma histories (Brewerton & Dennis, 2014; Harned et al., 2014). While future research is needed to examine the efficacy of emotion-focused interventions such as ICAT and DBT among individuals with comorbid

BN and SUD, the current findings suggest that the targeting of this potentially transdiagnostic maintenance mechanism may be clinically-beneficial for individuals presenting with both binge-eating and substance use pathology, particularly when reporting a history of childhood maltreatment.

Conclusions

In sum, the current study indicates that among women with bulimic-spectrum disorders, emotional abuse and emotional neglect in childhood may lead to emotion dysregulation and impulsivity, respectively. Further, emotion dysregulation appears to increase the risk for problematic substance use in this population, suggesting that individuals with bulimic pathology may use drugs and/or alcohol to help manage or escape from distressing emotions. Results indicate that emotion dysregulation may be an important mechanism linking a history of childhood emotional maltreatment to later eating and substance use problems. Therefore, treatments, which seek to bolster emotion regulation skills among individuals with co-occurring bulimic-spectrum and substance use concerns may prove beneficial, though continued work is needed to evaluate emotion-focused therapies in this group.

Funding

This research was supported in part by John Simon Guggenheim Foundation; [grants 1 R01-MH/DK58820, NIH 1 R01-DK61973, NIH 1 R01-MH59100, NIH 1 R01-MH66287, NIH P30-DK50456, K02 MH65919, R01 MH 59234, and NIMH T32 MH082761] from the National Institutes of Health; Walden W. and Jean Young Shaw Foundation; University of Missouri Research Council.

ORCID

Vivienne M. Hazzard http://orcid.org/0000-0003-3933-1766
Kathryn E. Smith http://orcid.org/0000-0001-6555-0060
Daniel Le Grange http://orcid.org/0000-0001-7293-9496

References

Accurso, E. C., Wonderlich, S. A., Crosby, R. D., Smith, T. L., Klein, M. H., Mitchell, J. E., Crow, S. J., Berg, K. C., & Peterson, C. B. (2016). Predictors and moderators of treatment outcome in a randomized clinical trial for adults with symptoms of bulimia nervosa. *Journal of Consulting and Clinical Psychology*, *84*(2), 178–184. https://doi.org/10.1037/ccp0000073

American Psychiatric Association. (1994). *Diagnostic and statistical manual of mental disorders* (4th ed.). Author.

American Psychiatric Association. (2013). *Diagnostic and statistical manual of mental disorders* (5^h ed.). Author.

Anestis, M. D., Peterson, C. B., Bardone-Cone, A. M., Klein, M. H., Mitchell, J. E., Crosby, R. D., Wonderlich, S. A., Crow, S. J., Le Grange, D., & Joiner, T. E. (2009). Affective lability and impulsivity in a clinical sample of women with bulimia nervosa: The role of affect in severely dysregulated behavior. *International Journal of Eating Disorders, 42* (3), 259–266. https://doi.org/10.1002/eat.20606

Bahji, A., Mazhar, M. N., Hudson, C. C., Nadkarni, P., MacNeil, B. A., & Hawken, E. (2019). Prevalence of substance use disorder comorbidity among individuals with eating disorders: A systematic review and meta-analysis. *Psychiatry Research, 273*, 58–66. https://doi.org/10.1016/j.psychres.2019.01.007

Baker, J. H., Mitchell, K. S., Neale, M. C., & Kendler, K. S. (2010). Eating disorder symptomatology and substance use disorders: Prevalence and shared risk in a population based twin sample. *International Journal of Eating Disorders, 43*(7), 648–658. https://doi.org/10.1002/eat.20856

Bardone-Cone, A. M., Maldonado, C. R., Crosby, R. D., Mitchell, J. E., Wonderlich, S. A., Joiner, T. E., Jr., Crow, S. J., Peterson, C. B., Klein, M. H., & Le Grange, D. (2008). Revisiting differences in individuals with bulimia nervosa with and without a history of anorexia nervosa: Eating pathology, personality, and maltreatment. *International Journal of Eating Disorders, 41*(8), 697–704. https://doi.org/10.1002/eat.20567

Barratt, E. (1959). Anxiety and impulsiveness related to psychomotor efficiency. *Perceptual and Motor Skills, 9*(3), 191–198. https://doi.org/10.2466/PMS.9.3.191-198

Bernstein, D. P., & Fink, L. (1998). *Chilhood trauma questionnaire: A retrospective self-report manual.* Pearson.

Bernstein, D. P., Stein, J. A., Newcomb, M. D., Walker, E., Pogge, D., Ahluvalia, T., Stokes, J., Handelsman, L., Medrano, M., Desmond, D., & Zule, W. (2003). Development and validation of a brief screening version of the childhood trauma questionnaire. *Child Abuse and Neglect, 27*(2), 169–190. https://doi.org/10.1016/S0145-2134(02)00541-0

Brewerton, T. D., & Dennis, A. B. (2014). *Eating disorders, addictions and substance use disorders: Research, clinical and treatment perspectives.* Springer-Verlag Publishing.

Brownstone, L. M., Fitzsimmons-Craft, E. E., Wonderlich, S. A., Joiner, T. E., Le Grange, D., Mitchell, J. E., Crow, S. J., Peterson, C. B., Crosby, R. D., Klein, M. H., & Bardone-Cone, A. M. (2013). Hard exercise, affect lability, and personality among individuals with bulimia nervosa. Eating behaviors, 14(4), 413–419. https://doi.org/10.1016/j.eatbeh.2013.07.004

Burns, E. E., Fischer, S., Jackson, J. L., & Harding, H. G. (2012). Deficits in emotion regulation mediate the relationship between childhood abuse and later eating disorder symptoms. *Child Abuse and Neglect, 36*(1), 32–39. https://doi.org/10.1016/j.chiabu.2011.08.005

Caslini, M., Bartoli, F., Crocamo, C., Dakanalis, A., Clerici, M., & Carrà, G. (2016). Disentangling the association between child abuse and eating disorders: A systematic review and meta-analysis. *Psychosomatic Medicine, 78*(1), 79–90. https://doi.org/10.1097/PSY.0000000000000233

Centers for Disease Control and Prevention. (2020). *Defining adult overweight and obesity.* https://www.cdc.gov/obesity/adult/defining.html

Cloitre, M., Miranda, R., Stovall-McClough, K. C., & Han, H. (2005). Beyond PTSD: Emotion regulation and interpersonal problems as predictors of functional impairment in survivors of childhood abuse. *Behavior Therapy, 36*(2), 119–124. https://doi.org/10.1016/S0005-7894(05)80060-7

Cohen, J. (1988). *Statistical power analysis for the behavioral sciences.* Routledge Academic.

Crosby, R. D., Wonderlich, S. A., Engel, S. G., Simonich, H., Smyth, J., & Mitchell, J. E. (2009). Daily mood patterns and bulimic behaviors in the natural environment. *Behaviour and Research Therapy, 47*(3), 181–188. https://doi.org/10.1016/j.brat.2008.11.006

Dawe, S., & Mattick, R. P. (1997). *Review of diagnostic screening instruments for alcohol and other drug use and other psychiatric disorders*. Produced by the Australian Government Publishing Service.

Dennis, A. B., Pryor, T., & Brewerton, T. D. (2014). Integrated treatment principles and strategies for patients with eating disorders, substance use disorder, and addictions. In T. D. Brewerton & A. B. Dennis (Eds.), *Eating disorders, addictions and substance use disorders: Research, clinical and treatment perspectives* (pp. 461–489). Springer-Verlag Publishing.

Dennis, A. B., & Pryor, T. (2018). The complex relationship between eating disorders and substance use disorders: Clinical implications. In L. K. Anderson, S. B. Murray, & W. H. Kaye (Eds.), *Clinical handbook of complex and atypical eating disorders* (pp. 60–78). Oxford University Press.

Dick, D. M., Smith, G., Olausson, P., Mitchell, S. H., Leeman, R. F., O'Malley, S. S., & Sher, K. (2010). Understanding the construct of impulsivity and its relationship to alcohol use disorders. *Addiction Biology*, *15*(2), 217–226. https://doi.org/10.1111/j.1369-1600.2009.00190.x

Dworkin, E., Javdani, S., Verona, E., & Campbell, R. (2014). Child sexual abuse and disordered eating: The mediating role of impulsive and compulsive tendencies. *Psychology of Violence*, *4* (1), 21–36. https://doi.org/10.1037/a0031779

Elran-Barak, R., Sztainer, M., Goldschmidt, A. B., Crow, S. J., Peterson, C. B., Hill, L. L., Crosby, R. D., Powers, P., Mitchell, J. E., & Le Grange, D. (2015). Dietary restriction behaviors and binge eating in anorexia nervosa, bulimia nervosa and binge eating disorder: Trans-diagnostic examination of the restraint model. *Eating Behaviors*, *18*, 192–196. https://doi.org/10.1016/j.eatbeh.2015.05.012

Enoch, M.-A. (2011). The role of early life stress as a predictor for alcohol and drug dependence. *Psychopharmacology*, *214*(1), 17–31. https://doi.org/10.1007/s00213-010-1916-6

First, M. B., Spitzer, R. L., Gibbon, M., & Williams, J. B. (1995). *Structured clinical interview for DSM-IV-TR Axis I disorders: Patient Edition (SCID-I/P, version 2)*. New York State Psychiatric Research Institute, Biometrics Research Department.

Gregorowski, C., Seedat, S., & Jordaan, G. P. (2013). A clinical approach to the assessment and management of co-morbid eating disorders and substance use disorders. *BMC Psychiatry*, *13* (1). https://doi.org/10.1186/1471-244X-13-289

Harned, M. S., Korslund, K. E., & Linehan, M. M. (2014). A pilot randomized controlled trial of dialectical behavior therapy with and without the dialectical behavior therapy prolonged exposure protocol for suicidal and self-injuring women with borderline personality disorder and PTSD. *Behaviour Research and Therapy*, *55*, 7–17. https://doi.org/10.1016/j.brat.2014.01.008

Harrop, E. N., & Marlatt, G. A. (2010). The comorbidity of substance use disorders and eating disorders in women: Prevalence, etiology, and treatment. *Addictive Behaviors*, *35*(5), 392–398. https://doi.org/10.1016/j.addbeh.2009.12.016

Heatherton, T. F., & Baumeister, R. F. (1991). Binge eating as escape from self- awareness. *Psychological Bulletin*, *110*(1), 86–108. https://doi.org/10.1037/0033-2909.110.1.86

Kim, K., Mennen, F. E., & Trickett, P. K. (2017). Patterns and correlates of co-occurrence among multiple types of child maltreatment. *Child & Family Social Work*, *22*(1), 492–502. https://doi.org/10.1111/cfs.12268

Lavender, J. M., & Mitchell, J. E. (2015). Eating disorders and their relationship to impulsivity. *Current Treatment Options in Psychiatry*, *2*(4), 394–401. https://doi.org/10.1007/s40501-015-0061-6

Lavender, J. M., Wonderlich, S. A., Engel, S. G., Gordon, K. H., Kaye, W. H., & Mitchell, J. E. (2015). Dimensions of emotion dysregulation in anorexia nervosa and bulimia nervosa: A conceptual review of the empirical literature. *Clinical Psychology Review, 40*, 111–122. https://doi.org/10.1016/j.cpr.2015.05.010

Lee, R. S. C., Hoppenbrouwers, S., & Franken, I. (2019). A systematic meta-review of impulsivity and compulsivity in addictive behaviors. *Neuropsychology Review, 29*(1), 14–26. https://doi.org/10.1007/s11065-019-09402-x

Linehan, M. M. (1993). *Cognitive-behavioral treatment of borderline personality disorder.* Guilford Press.

Linehan, M. M. (2015). *DBT skills training manual, 2nd ed.* Guilford Press.

Liu, R. T. (2019). Childhood maltreatment and impulsivity: A meta-analysis and recommendations for future study. *Journal of Abnormal Child Psychology, 47*(2), 221–243. https://doi.org/10.1007/s10802-018-0445-3

Livesley, J. W., Jackson, D. N., & Schroeder, M. L. (1992). Factorial structure of traits delineating personality disorders in clinical and general population samples. *Journal of Abnormal Psychology, 101*(3), 432–440. https://doi.org/10.1037/0021-843X.101.3.432

Livesley, J. W., Jang, K. L., & Vernon, P. A. (1998). Phenotypic and genetic structure of traits delineating personality disorder. *Archives of General Psychiatry, 55*(10), 941–948. https://doi.org/10.1001/archpsyc.55.10.941

Livesley, W. J., & Jackson, D. N. (2009). *Dimensional assessment of personality pathology – basic questionnaire: Technical manual.* Sigma Assessment Systems.

Mills, P., Newman, E. F., Cossar, J., & Murray, G. (2015). Emotional maltreatment and disordered eating in adolescents: Testing the mediating role of emotion regulation. *Child Abuse & Neglect, 39*, 156–166. https://doi.org/10.1016/J.CHIABU.2014.05.011

Molendijk, M. L., Hoek, H. W., Brewerton, T. D., & Elzinga, B. M. (2017). Childhood maltreatment and eating disorder pathology: A systematic review and dose-response meta-analysis. *Psychological Medicine, 47*(8), 1402–1416. https://doi.org/10.1017/S0033291716003561

Moulton, S. J., Newman, E., Power, K., Swanson, V., & Day, K. (2015). Childhood trauma and eating psychopathology: A mediating role for dissociation and emotion dysregulation? *Child Abuse & Neglect, 39*, 167–174. https://doi.org/10.1016/j.chiabu.2014.07.003

Moustafa, A. A., Parkes, D., Fitzgerald, L., Underhill, D., Garami,J., Levy-Gigi, E., Stramecki, F., Valikhani, A., Frydecka, D., & Misiak, B. (2021). The relationship between childhood trauma, early-life stress, and alcohol and drug use, abuse, and addiction: An integrative review. Current Psychology: A Journal for DiversePerspectives on Diverse Psychological Issues, 40, 579–584. https://doi.org/10.1007/s12144-018-9973-9

National Center on Addiction and Substance Abuse (CASA) at Columbia University (2003). *Food for thought: Substance abuse and eating disorders.* http://www.casacolumbia.org/templates/Publications_Reports.aspx

Oshri, A., Kogan, S. M., Kwon, J. A., Wickrama, K. A. S., Vanderbroek, L., Palmer, A. A., & MacKillop, J. (2018). Impulsivity as a mechanism linking child abuse and neglect with substance use in adolescence and adulthood. *Development and Psychopathology, 30*(2), 417–435. https://doi.org/10.1017/S0954579417000943

Patton, J. H., Stanford, M. S., & Barratt, E. S. (1995). Factor structure of the barratt impulsiveness scale. *Journal of Clinical Psychology, 51*(6), 768–774. https://doi.org/10.1002/1097-4679(199511)51:6<768::AID-JCLP2270510607>3.0.CO;2-1

Peterson, C. B., Berg, K. C., Crosby, R. D., Lavender, J. M., Accurso, E. C., Ciao, A. C., Smith, T. L., Klein, M., Mitchell, J. E., Crow, S. J., & Wonderlich, S. A. (2017). The effects of psychotherapy treatment on outcome in bulimia nervosa: Examining indirect effects through emotion regulation, self-directed behavior, and self-discrepancy within the mediation model. *International Journal of Eating Disorders, 50*(6), 636–647. https://doi.org/10.1002/eat.22669

Pollak, S. D. (2008). Mechanisms linking early experience and the emergence of emotions: Illustrations from the study of maltreated children. *Current Directions in Psychological Science, 17*(6), 370–375. https://doi.org/10.1111/j.1467-8721.2008.00608.x

Selzer, M. L. (1971). The michigan alcoholism screening test: The quest for a new diagnostic instrument. *American Journal of Psychiatry, 127*(12), 1653–1658. https://doi.org/10.1176/ajp.127.12.1653

Sloan, E., Hall, K., Moulding, R., Bryce, S., Mildred, H., & Staiger, P. K. (2017). Emotion regulation as a transdiagnostic treatment construct across anxiety, depression, substance, eating and borderline personality disorders: A systematic review. *Clinical Psychology Review, 57*, 141–163. https://doi.org/10.1016/j.cpr.2017.09.002

Smith, K. E., Mason, T. B., Johnson, J. S., Lavender, J. M., & Wonderlich, S. A. (2018). A systematic review of reviews of neurocognitive functioning in eating disorders: The state-of-the-literature and future directions. *International Journal of Eating Disorders, 51*(8), 798–821. https://doi.org/10.1002/eat.22929

Smolak, L., & Murnen, S. K. (2002). A meta-analytic examination of the relationship between child sexual abuse and eating disorders. *International Journal of Eating Disorders, 31*(2), 136–150. https://doi.org/10.1002/eat.10008

Soenke, M., Hahn, K. S., Tull, M. T., & Gratz, K. L. (2010). Exploring the relationship between childhood abuse and analogue generalized anxiety disorder: The mediating role of emotion dysregulation. *Cognitive Therapy and Research, 34*(5), 401–412. https://doi.org/10.1007/s10608-009-9264-8

Spinhoven, P., Penninx, B. W., Hickendorff, M., Van Helmert, A. M., Bernstein, D. P., & Elzinga, B. M. (2014). Childhood trauma questionnaire: Factor structure, measurement invariance, and validity across emotional disorders. *Psychological Assesment, 26*(3), 717–729. https://doi.org/10.1037/pas0000002

Steiger, H., Koerner, N., Engelberg, M. J., Israël, M., Ying Kin, N. M. K., & Young, S. N. (2001). Self-destructiveness and serotonin function in bulimia nervosa. *Psychiatry Research, 103*(1), 15–26. https://doi.org//10.1016/S0165-1781(01)00264-5

Trottier, K., & MacDonald, D. E. (2017). Update on psychological trauma, other severe adverse experiences and eating disorders: State of the research and future directions. *Current Psychiatry Reports, 19*(8), 45. https://doi.org/10.1007/s11920-017-0806-6

Weiss, N. H., Schick, M. R., Contractor, A. A., & Dixon-Gordon, K. L. (2019). Posttraumatic stress disorder and substance use: Identifying the underlying role of difficulties regulating positive emotions. *Addictive Behaviors, 96(5)*, 119–126. https://doi.org/10.1016/j.addbeh.2019.04.029

Westermeyer, J., Yargic, I., & Thuras, P. (2009). Michigan assessment-screening test for alcohol and drugs (MAST/AD): Evaluation in a clinical sample. *American Journal on Addictions, 13*(2), 151–162. https://doi.org/10.1080/10550490490435948

Whiteside, S. P., & Lynam, D. R. (2001). The five factor model and impulsivity: Using a structural model of personality to understand impulsivity. *Personality and Individual Differences, 30*(4), 669–689. https://doi.org/10.1016/S0191-8869(00)00064-7

Wonderlich, S. A., Crosby, R. D., Joiner, T., Peterson, C. B., Bardone-Cone, A., Klein, M., Crow, S., Mitchell, J. E., Le Grange, D., Steiger, H., Kolden, G., Johnson, F., & Vrshek, S. (2005). Personality subtyping and bulimia nervosa: Psychopathological and genetic correlates. *Psychological Medicine, 35*(5), 649–657. https://doi.org/10.1017/S0033291704004234

Wonderlich, S. A., Peterson, C. B., & Smith, T. L. (2015). *Integrative cognitive-affective therapy for bulimia nervosa: A treatment manual.* Guilford Publications.

World Health Organization. (2020). *Prevalence of underweight among adults.* https://www.who.int/data/gho/indicator-metadata-registry/imr-details/4804

Part III

Developing effective ED-PTSD treatments

Posttraumatic stress disorder and eating disorders: maintaining mechanisms and treatment targets

Karen S. Mitchell, Erica R. Scioli, Tara Galovski, Perry L. Belfer, and Zafra Cooper

ABSTRACT

Many individuals with lifetime histories of eating disorders (EDs) report exposure to interpersonal trauma and posttraumatic stress disorder (PTSD). However, this relationship is not well-understood, and there are no established, evidence-based therapies for the concurrent treatment of EDs and PTSD. This review focuses on studies of the mechanisms associating trauma exposure and/or PTSD with EDs. Possible mechanisms of the trauma-ED association identified from the literature include self-criticism, low self-worth, guilt, shame, depression, anxiety, emotion dysregulation, anger, and impulsivity/compulsivity. ED behaviors may be used as coping strategies to manage PTSD symptoms and negative affect. Avoidance of hyperarousal symptoms by engaging in binge eating, purging, and/or restriction may serve to maintain both the ED as well as the PTSD. Given the evidence of the bidirectional relationship between EDs and PTSD, we describe an integrated cognitive behavioral theory that may account for the persistence of comorbid PTSD and EDs. The integrated model is based on the theoretical models that underpin existing evidence-based treatments for PTSD and ED and incorporates many of the potential mechanisms highlighted to date. The primary aim of the model is to identify potential treatment targets as well as elucidate future directions for research.

Clinical Implications

- Eating disorders and posttraumatic stress disorder frequently co-occur
- There are no established integrated treatments for these two conditions
- Several psychosocial mechanisms may account for this association
- Understanding mechanisms may help identify treatment targets

Many individuals with lifetime histories of eating disorders (EDs) report exposure to interpersonal forms of trauma, including childhood physical abuse, physical intimate partner violence, and sexual assault (Mitchell, Mazzeo et al., 2012). Further, in a nationally representative U.S. sample

(*N*=5,692), a significant proportion of individuals with bulimia nervosa (BN; 39.8% of women, 66.2% of men) and binge eating disorder (BED; 25.7% of women and 24.0% of men) reported a lifetime history of posttraumatic stress disorder (PTSD). In addition, 16.1% of women with lifetime anorexia nervosa (AN) endorsed lifetime PTSD (Mitchell et al., 2012). In this sample, we also found that substantial proportions of those affected likely met criteria for both disorders concurrently. Specifically, 43.8% of those meeting criteria for BN in the past year and 23.6% of those with past year BED also met criteria for past year PTSD (unpublished data). The well-documented relationship between ED and PTSD symptoms/diagnoses raises interesting theoretical questions about the mechanisms responsible for their co-occurrence as well as related clinical questions about how these disorders should be treated when they co-occur.

Currently there are no established, evidence-based therapies for the concurrent treatment of EDs and PTSD (or indeed, for treating EDs and any comorbid condition). Further examination of the relationship between EDs and comorbid PTSD would not only advance our theoretical understanding of this comorbidity but would likely contribute to the development of treatments for these disorders when comorbid. Although the lifetime comorbidity of PTSD and EDs has been relatively well-established in the literature, data on the temporal relationship between the two disorders is scarce, and there have been few studies on the mechanisms that may account for their co-occurrence. The majority of studies have investigated variables that putatively link trauma exposure, rather than PTSD specifically, to EDs. As a result, this review focuses both on studies of the mechanisms associating trauma exposure and PTSD with EDs. Based on our review of this literature, we present a theoretical model that focuses on potential maintaining features that may account for the persistence of co-occurring EDs and PTSD. The primary aim of the model is to identify potential treatment targets as well as elucidate future directions for research.

Trauma exposure and PTSD and EDs

The association between childhood abuse and EDs has long been a focus of investigation. Retrospective case-control studies describing cases in which trauma preceded the onset of EDs have highlighted childhood physical and sexual abuse as likely risk factors (albeit non-specific) for AN, BN, and BED (Fairburn et al., 1999, 1998, 1997; Hilbert et al., 2014; Striegel-Moore et al., 2002). Similarly, a prospective study of the temporal onset of trauma exposures and EDs found that childhood adversity predicted the later onset of EDs among both male and female participants (Johnson et al., 2002).

As the majority of studies of trauma/PTSD and EDs have been cross-sectional or retrospective in nature and have not established temporal precedence, they do not determine risk factors but rather correlates (Jacobi et al., 2004). Several studies have found that childhood maltreatment was associated with increased self-criticism, which in turn was associated with multiple negative outcomes, including depression, non-suicidal self-injury, and body dissatisfaction (Dunkley et al., 2010; Glassman et al., 2007). In addition, a recent qualitative study found that disordered eating among trauma survivors was associated with low self-worth, guilt, and shame, and served as a form of self-punishment (Breland et al., 2017). Anxiety, depression, and alexithymia have also been identified as mediators of the cross-sectional association between childhood abuse and ED symptoms among women (Mazzeo et al., 2008), although only depression was a mediator of the association between childhood maltreatment and ED symptoms among men in these same data (Mitchell & Mazzeo, 2005). Maladaptive beliefs about trust, emotional inhibition, and effectiveness stemming from childhood abuse may be associated with ED symptoms as well (Feinson & Hornik-Lurie, 2016b; Groleau et al., 2012; Jenkins et al., 2013). As recently reviewed by Trottier and MacDonald (2017), other potential mechanisms of the trauma-ED association include emotion dysregulation, anger, and impulsivity/compulsivity.

Consistent with these co-occurring symptoms, there is evidence that PTSD itself may partly account for the association between trauma exposure and EDs (Brewerton, 2007; Holzer et al., 2008; Karr et al., 2013). For example, among women with histories of childhood and/or adulthood sexual assault, avoidance and hyperarousal symptoms of PTSD mediated the trauma-ED symptoms relation (Holzer et al., 2008). Recent studies of female veterans (Huston et al., 2019) and African American and African Caribbean women (Lucea et al., 2012) found that the association between intimate partner violence and ED symptoms was mediated by PTSD and depression symptoms.

Bidirectional relationship between Trauma/PTSD and EDs

Several potential maintaining mechanisms of the bidirectional relationship between trauma/PTSD and EDs have been identified in the literature. ED symptoms, particularly binge eating and purging, may serve a self-medication function or act as a coping strategy to mitigate PTSD symptoms. In support of this, Mitchell and Wolf (2016) found that a maladaptive form of emotion regulation mediated the association between PTSD and ED symptoms among male and female veterans. Avoidance, which is a symptom of PTSD and also common to EDs (e.g., in terms of avoiding emotions), may contribute to their co-occurrence (Trottier et al., 2016). For example, successful suppression of hyperarousal symptoms achieved by engaging in binge eating and purging (and possibly restriction) may serve to maintain both the ED as well as the PTSD. The need for control is also common to both PTSD and EDs. The perceived importance of controlling eating, weight, and shape is a core feature of EDs (Fairburn et al., 2003). PTSD is likely to develop when a traumatic event is perceived as "dangerous and uncontrollable" (Kushner et al., 1992). Perceived control over current or future trauma, through self or other blame, has been found to increase avoidance and undermine the recovery process.

A recent network analysis found three major pathways between EDs and PTSD, the strongest of which was between binge eating and irritability. Three PTSD symptoms (difficulty concentrating, trouble remembering aspects of the trauma, and sleep disturbance) were also associated with weight/shape dissatisfaction and difficulty concentrating due to preoccupation with food and body concerns. Body dissatisfaction was also linked to the PTSD symptoms of disturbing dreams and trouble remembering aspects of the trauma (Vanzhula et al., 2019). These results are consistent with previous findings that binge eating may serve to regulate or avoid emotions and also that trauma exposure/PTSD symptoms may lead to self-criticism of one's body (Dunkley et al., 2010; Heatherton & Baumeister, 1991).

Taken together, the literature suggests that there is a bidirectional relationship between EDs and PTSD. Based on these findings, we have developed an integrated cognitive behavioral theory that may account for the persistence of comorbid PTSD and EDs. The integrated model is based on the theoretical models that underpin existing evidence-based treatments for PTSD and ED. In the sections below, we present an overview of the cognitive behavioral models of both PTSD and EDs. We discuss their overlap and how we integrated research findings, reviewed above, as well as our clinical experience to develop this model.

Cognitive behavioral model of PTSD

The two leading treatments for PTSD, Prolonged Exposure (PE) and Cognitive Processing Therapy (CPT), are both grounded in cognitive behavioral theory, including the impact of trauma on information processing and memory function (Lang, 1977). Foa et al.'s (1989) emotional processing theory specifically informed the development of PE. According to this theory, a fear network is formed after exposure to a traumatic event. As this fear network develops, objectively safe stimuli (e.g., nighttime, loud noises, people who remind survivors of their perpetrator) become associated with danger. Avoidance of trauma reminders prevents the processing of trauma-related emotions that are necessary for recovery. In PE, emotional processing is achieved using in vivo exposure to trauma-related situations and imaginal exposure to the traumatic event (Foa et al., 2007).

The specific cognitive behavioral model underpinning CPT is heavily influenced by both information processing theory and cognitive theory. According to cognitive theory, individuals' interpretations of their traumatic experiences influence their emotional and behavioral responses to the trauma. Distorted beliefs cause distress; correcting these automatic thoughts to more accurately reflect reality leads to decreased distress and improved functioning (Beck, 1976). While a range of natural emotions (such as fear, anger, sadness) occur directly in response to the trauma, non-intrinsic emotions such as shame and guilt may also develop as a result of inaccurate beliefs about why the traumatic event occurred (Resick et al., 2017). The goal of CPT is arriving at balanced, accurate conclusions about why the trauma happened (e.g., "It was my perpetrator's fault") and balanced current and future beliefs about oneself, the world and others (e.g., "Not all men are dangerous"). Accessing and expressing the natural affect associated with the trauma allows the emotions to dissipate naturally, and challenging inaccurate beliefs decreases the non-intrinsic emotions and intrusive reminders (Resick et al., 2017).

Cognitive behavioral model of ED maintenance

The transdiagnostic theory of EDs considers the over-evaluation of weight, shape, eating, and their control, as central to maintaining EDs. The over-evaluation often arises in the context of a desire to be in control and feelings of low self-worth. Dietary restraint and restriction, as well as other forms of weight control behavior (e.g., excessive exercise and purging), preoccupation with thoughts about eating, shape, and weight, and body checking, stem directly from this over-evaluation (Fairburn et al., 2003). Extreme attempts to control weight may lead to low weight and/or binge eating. Binge eating results in further attempts to manage weight by dieting/fasting/excessive exercise/purging, and further intensifies concerns about controlling weight, shape and eating. Interpersonal event- and mood-related triggers of binge eating or extreme dietary restriction can also contribute to the persistence of the ED.

Enhanced Cognitive-Behavioral Therapy (CBT-E; Fairburn, 2008) is a leading treatment for EDs derived from the transdiagnostic theory of the processes that maintain EDs. Treatment is guided by a personalized formulation of the patient's difficulties that identifies the particular processes maintaining the disorder. Patients are encouraged to make changes in the way they behave and to understand and reflect on the effects and implications of these changes. CBT-E integrates cognitive and behavioral procedures together with relevant education to help patients de-center from their eating problems, identify their ED mindset, and eventually manage it, adaptively. Thus regular eating and the challenging of inflexible dietary rules (including avoided foods) reduces binge eating and dietary restriction and challenges patients' assumptions and fears about weight gain. Regular weighing and education about the interpretation of weight fluctuations reduces preoccupation with weight and shape and avoidance of knowing one's weight. The reduction of body checking and comparison-making modifies the over-evaluation of weight and shape and their control.

Cognitive behavioral theory of comorbid PTSD and EDs

Given that cognitive behavioral theory serves as the basis of empirically validated treatments for PTSD and EDs, we believe these two complementary theories of symptom maintenance can be integrated to understand the comorbidity of PTSD and ED. The overlap between the underlying mechanisms of CPT and CBT-E supports CPT as an excellent candidate for an integrated

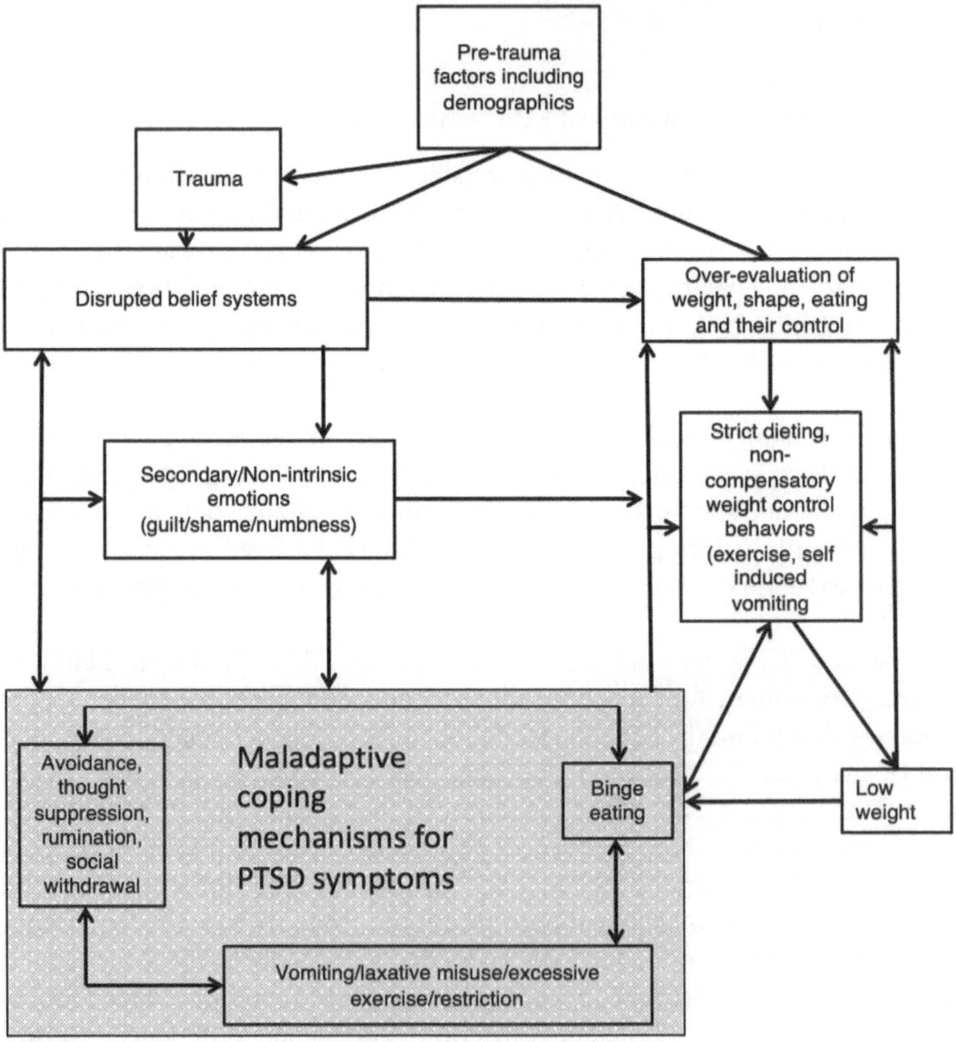

Figure 1. Integrated congnitive behavioral theory of posttraumatic stress disorder and the transdiagnostic theory of eating disorders.

model of recovery. We have developed a model (Figure 1) to explain the interaction and bidirectional nature of co-occurring PTSD and ED symptoms and thus guide the development of treatment. This model illustrates the mechanisms that maintain each disorder individually and the hypothesized functional linkages between the symptoms of the two disorders. It is inherently flexible so as to reflect the complexity of comorbidity, providing the clinician with the opportunity to derive an individualized formulation of each patient's difficulties that would serve to guide treatment.

Associations between trauma-related distorted beliefs and shape and weight concerns

Trauma-related distorted beliefs and low self-worth may contribute to the onset of or enhance pre-existing concerns about controlling shape and weight. For example, women and men with histories of sexual assault report more negative images of their physical selves (Campbell & Soeken, 1999; Talmon & Ginzburg, 2018). Childhood emotional abuse may result in the belief that one is flawed or inadequate, and the development of self-critical beliefs (Feinson & Hornik-Lurie, 2016b; Groleau et al., 2012). A recent study found that beliefs related to mistrust mediated the association between childhood emotional abuse and drive for thinness, and beliefs related to abandonment mediated the association between childhood sexual abuse and bulimic symptoms (Jenkins et al., 2013).

Associations between distorted beliefs, non-intrinsic emotions, and ED behaviors

Beliefs related to self-criticism, low self-worth, or self-punishment and accompanying non-intrinsic emotions, in the context of over-evaluation of weight and shape, may lead to dieting and other weight loss behaviors. For example, childhood sexual abuse may contribute to a sense of a lack of control over one's body (Dworkin et al., 2014). Dietary restriction may serve as a means to regain a sense of control following trauma exposure (Trim et al., 2017).

Associations between emotion dysregulation and ED behaviors

Emotion dysregulation, anger, and dissociation are symptoms or associated features of PTSD that also have been identified as mechanisms of the trauma-ED association (Feinson & Hornik-Lurie, 2016a; Mills et al., 2015; Moulton et al., 2015). For example, anger has been found to precede binge eating, which may become a way of coping with this emotion and accompanying self-criticism. Although dysfunctional in the long term, binge eating may be reinforced as a coping mechanism due to its short term ability to blunt emotions (Feinson & Hornik-Lurie, 2016a). Disordered eating behaviors may also be used as a way to dissociate from negative cognitions and affect (Mills et al., 2015). Thus, while binge eating may initially develop in response to restraint and restriction, it may subsequently serve to "numb" emotions and decrease emotional arousal. Similarly purging may also serve to regulate emotions and thus be reinforced (Engelberg et al., 2007; Heatherton & Baumeister, 1991). Dietary restriction may also serve an affect regulation function by reducing ambiguity and providing simplified rules for daily function (Vitousek & Hollon, 1990). In summary, ED symptoms may be extensively reinforced by their function of reducing negative self-awareness and emotion dysregulation associated with PTSD symptoms.

Integrated treatment

To date, there are no specific treatments for addressing comorbid EDs and PTSD, nor are there clear guidelines about whether they should be treated together in an integrated fashion, or sequentially (and if so, then in what order?). The bidirectional interactions between the two disorders outlined above suggest that an integrated treatment might be optimal to address the full range of processes that contribute to the persistence of these disorders. Further, this may avoid patients presenting to ED or PTSD specialty clinics and being excluded from treatment or being told to seek it for one or other disorder elsewhere first (Trim et al., 2017).

The case for an integrated treatment rather than mono-therapies for either EDs or PTSD alone is further strengthened by previous research. PTSD is best treated with a trauma-focused intervention (*VA/DoD, 2017*) that is not part of standard evidence-based ED approaches, and PTSD treatment alone may not be effective in the case of EDs (Mitchell, Wells et al., 2012). Further, the literature from other fields such as substance use disorders, which are comorbid with both EDs and PTSD, suggests that integrated treatments are superior to mono-therapies (Kelly & Daley, 2013).

Given the functional links between ED and PTSD symptoms described above, our model suggests that the majority of cases would benefit from integrated treatment. However, there are several additional factors to consider, including patient preference. In some cases, ED treatment, or at least medical and symptom stabilization or weight restoration, would need to come first (Academy for Eating Disorders, 2016; Belfer et al., 2005). Or, PTSD treatment may need to be stopped temporarily if the ED worsens significantly and the health of the patient is compromised, in order to focus on the ED (Becker & Zayfert, 2001).

Only one published pilot study has investigated a combined partly sequential treatment for comorbid EDs and PTSD. Trottier and colleagues (Trottier, Monson, Wonderlich, Olmsted et al., 2017) implemented a version of CPT with elements of CBT-E in a non-controlled trial of 10 patients who had recently completed inpatient or intensive outpatient ED treatment. Patients first received intensive ED treatment for an average of 12.6 weeks and then received an additional 16 therapy sessions. The first three of these sessions focused on ED treatment maintenance, and the remaining sessions included CPT for PTSD integrated with ED treatment. Behavioral remission was defined in this study as ≤ 1 binge/purge episode in the past month and/or weight restoration to body mass index of ≥ 19. Remission of cognitive ED symptoms was operationalized as achieving an Eating Disorder Examination-Questionnaire global score within one standard deviation of community norms. PTSD remission was defined as no longer meeting diagnostic criteria for PTSD according to the Clinician Administered PTSD Scale-5. The authors found that 80.0% of participants experienced reliable PTSD improvements/ PTSD remission, while also maintaining ED behavioral remission. These very preliminary findings suggest that combining an evidence-based PTSD treatment with an evidence-based ED treatment may hold promise for treating these complex conditions. However, it should be noted that this was a fairly long treatment including an initial intensive ED treatment component.

Conclusions

Our model allows us to explain the interrelationships among PTSD and ED symptoms and the need to address symptoms of both disorders together. This model provides a framework for formulating the impact of the trauma on the patient's over-evaluation of weight and shape, and the extent to which binge eating and compensatory weight control behaviors are associated with PTSD symptoms. It highlights the need to address maladaptive beliefs about the trauma and their relation to body image and eating as well as the over-evaluation and its potential impact on PTSD symptoms. Targeting thoughts keeping the patient "stuck," as well as those maintaining ED behaviors, and replacing these thoughts with healthier beliefs and ways of evaluating oneself, would potentially address the PTSD as well as the ED.

The current model also points to specific cognitive behavioral interventions to address the role of PTSD with respect to the function of severe dietary restriction, binge eating, and purging behaviors (e.g., self-medication or avoidance in response to PTSD). PTSD-related changes in eating symptoms could be targeted by identifying the occurrence of the triggering events, resultant aversive moods, cognitive appraisal of events and moods, and use of dysfunctional mood modulatory behavior. ED treatment includes establishing regular eating in order to disrupt the cycle of dieting, binge eating, and purging. However, if these behaviors are also serving as maladaptive emotion regulation strategies for those with PTSD, they may be more resistant to change. As a result, targeting their role in maintaining the PTSD, as well as identifying healthier ways of coping, may contribute to improving treatment of the ED symptoms. In turn, providing psychoeducation about the maintaining role of avoidance, and using interventions to reduce avoidance and blunting of emotions, may contribute to promoting healthy processing of emotions required for the treatment of PTSD. This will also further decrease the use of ED behaviors as avoidance.

Future directions

The studies reviewed in this paper suggest two major areas of future research. First, longitudinal studies, using well-validated assessment instruments, are necessary to better elucidate the relationship between PTSD and EDs. Such studies should explore a range of risk factors for the two disorders, paying particular attention to the timing and sequencing of the disorders. For example, in contrast to those who over-evaluate weight and shape and engage in disordered eating to achieve an ideal body shape, others may develop ED symptoms such as binge eating or excessive exercise in order to appear heavier or more muscular to protect themselves from future assault (Breland et al., 2017; Felitti, 1993; Strother et al., 2012). This "alternate pathway" to the development of EDs following trauma exposure may be particularly relevant for men. Given gender differences in PTSD and EDs, it is important to explore gender similarities and differences in these models.

Second, the high rates of comorbidity between PTSD and EDs and the lack of current guidelines as how to best treat co-occurring PTSD and EDs underscore the need for further investigation. Support for treatment integration comes from recent findings that, among patients with BED, a higher perceived impact of the traumatic event, rather than the number of traumatic events experienced, negatively predicted remission during treatment (Serra et al., 2020). Further, Trottier found that comorbid PTSD predicted dropout from an intensive day hospital ED treatment program among a sample of women with BN or other specified feeding or eating disorder (Trottier, 2020).

Further study is needed to investigate the exact form that an integrated treatment should take, whether it should be fully integrated or partially sequential, such as was explored in Trottier and colleagues' pilot study (Trottier, Monson, Wonderlich, Olmsted et al., 2017). Another possible partially sequential approach would be to use modular CBT-E. This would involve a standard ED intervention in the first stage of treatment (see Fairburn, 2008) and then incorporating a PTSD treatment module in the main treatment intervention phase, the point at which CBT-E is individualized in accordance with the patient's particular presenting difficulties.

Although we focus here on integrating CPT and CBT-E, there are other treatments that may be effective for treating comorbid EDs and PTSD, including exposure-based treatments. PE is strongly supported as a front-line treatment for PTSD (*VA/DoD, 2017*), and there are elements of exposure present in CBT for EDs, including exposure to avoided foods and breaking one's dietary rules (Black Becker & Waller, 2016). Thus, an integrated exposure-based treatment for comorbid EDs and PTSD may be another promising area of future research.

In sum, EDs are serious psychiatric conditions that are often difficult to treat, and trauma exposure may be a barrier to recovery from EDs (Trottier, Monson, Wonderlich, MacDonald et al., 2017). PTSD diagnosis may predict treatment drop-out as well (Trottier, 2020), underscoring the need for improved treatment approaches for these comorbid conditions. We have provided a framework for understanding the interaction between PTSD and EDs that provides a first step towards establishing the need for an integrated treatment and outlining the possible targets of such a treatment.

Acknowledgments

The contents of this article do not represent the views of the U.S. Department of Veterans Affairs or the United States Government.

ORCID

Karen S. Mitchell http://orcid.org/0000-0002-1516-7239
Perry L. Belfer http://orcid.org/0000-0002-0518-8394

References

Academy for Eating Disorders. (2016). *Critical points for early recognition and medical risk management in the care of individuals with eating disorders.* http://www.nyeatingdisorders.org/pdf/AED%20Medical%20Management%20Guide%203rd%20Edition.pdf

Beck, A. T. (1976). *Cognitive therapy and the emotional disorders.* International Universities Press.

Becker, C. B., & Zayfert, C. (2001). Integrating DBT-cased techniques and concepts to facilitate exposure treatment for PTSD. *Cognitive and Behavioral Practice*, *8*(2), 107–122. https://doi.org/10.1016/S1077-7229(01)80017-1

Belfer, P., Warrenski, J., & Gomberg, R. (2005). *Eating disorders: Levels of care criteria* [Clinical document]. Newton-Wellesley Eating Disorders and Behavioral Medicine.

Black Becker, C., & Waller, G. (2016). Exposure-based strategies in treating eating disorders, the use of. In T. Wade (Ed.), *Encyclopedia of feeding and eating disorders* (pp. 1–6). Springer Nature Singapore Pte Ltd.

Breland, J. Y., Donalson, R., Dinh, J. V., & Maguen, S. (2017). Trauma exposure and disordered eating: A qualitative study. *Women & Health*, *58*(2), 160–174. https://doi.org/10.1080/03630242.2017.1282398

Brewerton, T. D. (2007). Eating disorders, trauma, and comorbidity: Focus on PTSD. *Eating Disorders: The Journal of Treatment & Prevention*, *15*(4), 285–304. https://doi.org/10.1080/10640260701454311

Campbell, J. C., & Soeken, K. L. (1999). Forced sex and intimate partner violence: Effects on women's risk and women's health. *Violence Against Women*, *5*(9), 1017–1035. https://doi.org/10.1177/10778019922181608

Dunkley, D. M., Masheb, R. M., & Grilo, C. M. (2010). Childhood maltreatment, depressive symptoms, and body dissatisfaction in patients with binge eating disorder: The mediating role of self-criticism. *International Journal of Eating Disorders*, *43*(3), 274–281. https://doi.org/10.1002/eat.20796

Dworkin, E., Javdani, S., Verona, E., & Campbell, R. (2014). Child sexual abuse and disordered eating: The mediating role of impulsive and compulsive tendencies. *Psychology of Violence*, *4* (1), 21–36. https://doi.org/10.1037/a0031779

Engelberg, M. J., Steiger, H., Gauvin, L., & Wonderlich, S. A. (2007). Binge antecedents in bulimic syndromes: An examination of dissociation and negative affect. *International Journal of Eating Disorders*, *40*(6), 531–536. https://doi.org/10.1002/eat.20399

Fairburn, C. G. (2008). *Cognitive Behavior Therapy and Eating Disorders*. The Guilford Press.

Fairburn, C. G., Cooper, Z., Doll, H. A., & Welch, S. L. (1999). Risk factors for anorexia nervosa: Three integrated case-control comparisons. *Archives of General Psychiatry*, *56*(5), 468–476. https://doi.org/10.1001/archpsyc.56.5.468

Fairburn, C. G., Cooper, Z., & Shafran, R. (2003). Cognitive behaviour therapy for eating disorders: A "transdiagnostic" theory and treatment. *Behaviour Research and Therapy*, *41* (5), 509–528. https://doi.org/10.1016/S0005-7967(02)00088-8

Fairburn, C. G., Doll, H. A., Welch, S. L., Hay, P. J., Davies, B. A., & O'Connor, M. E. (1998). Risk factors for binge eating disorder: A community-based, case-control study. *Archives of General Psychiatry*, *55*(5), 425–432. https://doi.org/10.1001/archpsyc.55.5.425

Fairburn, C. G., Welch, S. L., Doll, H. A., Davies, B. A., & O'Connor, M. E. (1997). Risk factors for bulimia nervosa. A community-based case-control study. *Archives of General Psychiatry*, *54*(6), 509–517. https://doi.org/10.1001/archpsyc.1997.01830180015003

Feinson, M. C., & Hornik-Lurie, T. (2016a). Binge eating & childhood emotional abuse: The mediating role of anger. *Appetite*, *105*, 487–493. https://doi.org/10.1016/j.appet.2016.05.018

Feinson, M. C., & Hornik-Lurie, T. (2016b). "Not good enough:" Exploring self-criticism's role as a mediator between childhood emotional abuse & adult binge eating. *Eating Behaviors*, *23*, 1–6. https://doi.org/10.1016/j.eatbeh.2016.06.005

Felitti, V. J. (1993). Childhood sexual abuse, depression, and family dysfunction in adult obese patients: A case control study. *Southern Medical Journal*, *86*(7), 732–736. https://doi.org/10.1097/00007611-199307000-00002

Foa, E. B., Hembree, E. A., & Rothbaum, B. O. (2007). *Prolonged exposure therapy for PTSD: Emotional processing of traumatic experiences*. Oxford University Press.

Foa, E. B., Steketee, G., & Rothbaum, B. O. (1989). Behavioral/cognitive conceptualizations of posttraumatic stress disorder. *Behavior Therapy*, *20*, 155–176.

Glassman, L. H., Weierich, M. R., Hooley, J. M., Deliberto, T. L., & Nock, M. K. (2007). Child maltreatment, non-suicidal self-injury, and the mediating role of self-criticism. - PubMed—NCBI. *Behavior Research and Therapy*, *45*(10), 2483–2490. https://doi.org/10.1016/j.brat.2007.04.002

Groleau, P., Steiger, H., Bruce, K., Israel, M., Sycz, L., Ouellette, A.-S., & Badawi, G. (2012). Childhood emotional abuse and eating symptoms in bulimic disorders: An examination of possible mediating variables. *The International Journal of Eating Disorders*, *45*(3), 326–332. https://doi.org/10.1002/eat.20939

Heatherton, T. F., & Baumeister, R. F. (1991). Binge eating as escape from self-awareness. *Psychological Bulletin, 110*(1), 86–108. https://doi.org/10.1037/0033-2909.110.1.86

Hilbert, A., Pike, K. M., Goldschmidt, A. B., Wilfley, D. E., Fairburn, C. G., Dohm, F. A., Walsh, B. T., & Striegel Weissman, R. (2014). Risk factors across the eating disorders. *Psychiatry Research, 220*(1–2), 500–506. https://doi.org/10.1016/j.psychres.2014.05.054

Holzer, S. R., Uppala, S., Wonderlich, S. A., Crosby, R. D., & Simonich, H. (2008). Mediational significance of PTSD in the relationship of sexual trauma and eating disorders. *Child Abuse & Neglect, 32*(5), 561. https://doi.org/10.1016/j.chiabu.2007.07.011

Huston, J. C., Grillo, A. R., Iverson, K. M., & Mitchell, K. S. (2019). Associations between disordered eating and intimate partner violence mediated by depression and posttraumatic stress disorder symptoms in a female veteran sample. *General Hospital Psychiatry, 58*, 77–82. https://doi.org/10.1016/j.genhosppsych.2019.03.007

Jacobi, C., Hayward, C., de Zwaan, M., Kraemer, H. C., & Agras, W. S. (2004). Coming to terms with risk factors for eating disorders: Application of risk terminology and suggestions for a general taxonomy. *Psychological Bulletin, 130*(1), 19–65. https://doi.org/10.1037/0033-2909.130.1.19

Jenkins, P. E., Meyer, C., & Blissett, J. M. (2013). Childhood abuse and eating psychopathology: The mediating role of core beliefs. *Journal of Aggression, Maltreatment & Trauma, 22*(3), 248–261. https://doi.org/10.1080/10926771.2013.741665

Johnson, J. G., Cohen, P., Kasen, S., & Brook, J. S. (2002). Childhood adversities associated with risk for eating disorders or weight problems during adolescence or early adulthood. *American Journal of Psychiatry, 159*(3), 394–400. https://doi.org/10.1176/appi.ajp.159.3.394

Karr, T. M., Crosby, R. D., Cao, L., Engel, S. G., Mitchell, J. E., Simonich, H., & Wonderlich, S. (2013). Posttraumatic stress disorder as a moderator of the association between negative affect and bulimic symptoms: An ecological momentary assessment study. *Comprehensive Psychiatry, 54*(1), 61–69. https://doi.org/10.1016/j.comppsych.2012.05.011

Kelly, T. M., & Daley, D. C. (2013). Integrated treatment of substance use and psychiatric disorders. *Social Work in Public Health, 28*(3–4), 388–406. https://doi.org/10.1080/19371918.2013.774673

Kushner, M. G., Riggs, D. S., Foa, E. B., & Miller, S. M. (1992). Perceived controllability and the development of posttraumatic stress disorder (PTSD) in crime victims. *Behavior Research and Therapy, 31*(1), 105–110. https://doi.org/10.1016/0005-7967(93)90048-Y

Lang, P. J. (1977). Imagery in therapy: An information processing analysis of fear. *Behavior Therapy, 8*(5), 862–886. https://doi.org/10.1016/S0005-7894(77)80157-3

Lucea, M. B., Francis, L., Sabri, B., Campbell, J. C., & Campbell, D. W. (2012). Disordered eating among African American and African Caribbean women: The influence of intimate partner violence, depression, and PTSD. *Issues in Mental Health Nursing, 33*(8), 513–521. https://doi.org/10.3109/01612840.2012.687037

Mazzeo, S. E., Mitchell, K. S., & Williams, L. J. (2008). Anxiety, alexithymia, and depression as mediators of the association between childhood abuse and eating disordered behavior in African American and European American women. *Psychology of Women Quarterly, 32*(3), 267–280. https://doi.org/10.1111/j.1471-6402.2008.00435.x

Mills, P., Newman, E. F., Cossar, J., & Murray, G. (2015). Emotional maltreatment and disordered eating in adolescents: Testing the mediating role of emotion regulation. *Child Abuse & Neglect, 39*, 156–166. https://doi.org/10.1016/j.chiabu.2014.05.011

Mitchell, K. S., & Mazzeo, S. E. (2005). Mediators of the association between abuse and disordered eating in undergraduate men. *Eating Behaviors, 6*(4), 318–327. https://doi.org/10.1016/j.eatbeh.2005.03.004

Mitchell, K. S., Mazzeo, S. E., Schlesinger, M. R., Brewerton, T. D., & Smith, B. N. (2012). Comorbidity of partial and subthreshold ptsd among men and women with eating disorders in the national comorbidity survey-replication study. *The International Journal of Eating Disorders*, *45*(3), 307–315. https://doi.org/10.1002/eat.20965

Mitchell, K. S., Wells, S. Y., Mendes, A., & Resick, P. A. (2012). Treatment Improves Symptoms Shared by PTSD and Disordered Eating. *Journal of Traumatic Stress*, *25*(5), 535–542. https://doi.org/10.1002/jts.21737

Mitchell, K. S., & Wolf, E. J. (2016). PTSD, food addiction, and disordered eating in a sample of primarily older veterans: The mediating role of emotion regulation. *Psychiatry Research*, *243*, 23–29. https://doi.org/10.1016/j.psychres.2016.06.013

Moulton, S. J., Newman, E., Power, K., Swanson, V., & Day, K. (2015). Childhood trauma and eating psychopathology: A mediating role for dissociation and emotion dysregulation? *Child Abuse & Neglect*, *39*, 167–174. https://doi.org/10.1016/j.chiabu.2014.07.003

Resick, P. A., Monson, C. M., & Chard, K. M. (2017). *Cognitive processing therapy for PTSD: A comprehensive manual.* The Guilford Press.

Serra, R., Kiekens, G., Tarsitani, L., Vrieze, E., Bruffaerts, R., Loriedo, C., An, A., & Vanderlinden, J. (2020). The effect of trauma and dissociation on the outcome of cognitive behavioural therapy for binge eating disorder: A 6-month prospective study. *European Eating Disorders Review*,*28*(3), 309–317. https://doi.org/10.1002/erv.2722

Striegel-Moore, R. H., Dohm, F. A., Pike, K. M., Wilfley, D. E., & Fairburn, C. G. (2002). Abuse, bullying, and discrimination as risk factors for binge eating disorder. *American Journal of Psychiatry*, *159*(11), 1902–1907. https://doi.org/10.1176/appi.ajp.159.11.1902

Strother, E., Lemberg, R., Stanford, S. C., & Turberville, D. (2012). Eating disorders in men: Underdiagnosed, undertreated, and misunderstood. *Eating Disorders*, *20*(5), 346–355. https://doi.org/10.1080/10640266.2012.715512

Talmon, A., & Ginzburg, K. (2018). "Body self" in the shadow of childhood sexual abuse: The long-term implications of sexual abuse for male and female adult survivors. *Child Abuse & Neglect*, *76*, 416–425. https://doi.org/10.1016/j.chiabu.2017.12.004

Trim, J. G., Galovski, T. E., Wagner, A., & Brewerton, T. (2017). Treating ED-PTSD patients: A synthesis of the literature and new treatment directions. In L. K. Anderson, S. B. Murray, & W. H. Kaye (Eds.), *Clinical Handbook of Complex and Atypical Eating Disorders* (pp. 40–59). Oxford University Press.

Trottier, K. (2020). Posttraumatic stress disorder predicts non-completion of day hospital treatment for bulimia nervosa and other specified feeding/eating disorder. *European Eating Disorders Review, Epub Ahead of Print*, *28*(3), 343–350. https://doi.org/10.1002/erv.2723

Trottier, K., & MacDonald, D. E. (2017). Update on psychological trauma, other severe adverse experiences and eating disorders: State of the research and future research directions. *Current Psychiatry Reports*, *19*(8), 45. https://doi.org/10.1007/s11920-017-0806-6

Trottier, K., Monson, C. M., Wonderlich, S. A., MacDonald, D. E., & Olmsted, M. P. (2017). Frontline clinicians' perspectives on and utilization of trauma-focused therapy with individuals with eating disorders. *Eating Disorders*, *25*(1), 22–36. https://doi.org/10.1080/10640266.2016.1207456

Trottier, K., Monson, C. M., Wonderlich, S. A., & Olmsted, M. P. (2017). Initial findings from Project Recover: Overcoming co-occurring eating disorders and posttraumatic stress disorder through integrated treatment. *Journal of Traumatic Stress*, *30*(2), 173–177. https://doi.org/10.1002/jts.22176

Trottier, K., Wonderlich, S. A., Monson, C. M., Crosby, R. D., & Olmsted, M. P. (2016). Investigating posttraumatic stress disorder as a psychological maintaining factor of eating disorders. *International Journal of Eating Disorders*, *49*(5), 455–457. https://doi.org/10.1002/eat.22516

VA/DoD. (2017). *Clinical practice guideline for the management of posttraumatic stress disorder and acute stress.*

Vanzhula, I. A., Calebs, B., Fewell, L., & Levinson, C. A. (2019). Illness pathways between eating disorder and post-traumatic stress disorder symptoms: Understanding comorbidity with network analysis. *European Eating Disorders Review: The Journal of the Eating Disorders Association*, *27*(2), 147–160. https://doi.org/10.1002/erv.2634

Vitousek, K. B., & Hollon, S. D. (1990). The investigation of schematic content and processing in eating disorders. *Cognitive Therapy and Research*, *14*(2), 191–214. https://doi.org/10.1007/BF01176209

Integrating cognitive processing therapy for posttraumatic stress disorder with cognitive behavioral therapy for eating disorders in PROJECT RECOVER

Kathryn Trottier and Candice M. Monson

ABSTRACT

Posttraumatic stress disorder (PTSD) frequently co-occurs with eating disorders (ED) and is likely to be a powerful ED maintaining factor for a significant subgroup of individuals. The goal of PROJECT RECOVER is to develop and evaluate concurrent integrated treatment approaches for ED-PTSD to enable these individuals to recover from both their ED and PTSD. To date, we have trialed two approaches to concurrent/integrated treatment in PROJECT RECOVER: (1) concurrent delivery of Cognitive Processing Therapy (CPT) for PTSD to individuals receiving intensive ED treatment, and (2) delivery of a manualized individual cognitive-behavioral therapy (CBT) addressing both ED and PTSD (Integrated CBT for ED-PTSD) following a period of initial ED treatment. Interventions from both CBT for ED, and CPT for PTSD can be utilized and adapted to address the functional relationship between ED and PTSD, and promote full recovery from both disorders. Examples include integrating PTSD symptoms into the cognitive-behavioral individualized formulation of ED maintenance; integrating the ED into psychoeducation about PTSD maintenance; and identifying maladaptive beliefs that connect the ED to the trauma and/or PTSD. Emerging evidence suggests that CPT can be successfully integrated with CBT for ED.

Clinical Implications

- Interventions from both Cognitive-Behavioral Therapy (CBT) for eating disorders (ED), and Cognitive Processing Therapy (CPT) for posttraumatic stress disorder (PTSD) can be integrated to address the functional relationship between ED and PTSD, and promote full recovery from both disorders.
- Emerging evidence suggests that CPT can be effectively integrated with CBT for ED.

- There is good reason to believe that integrated concurrent treatment of ED-PTSD will be not only beneficial, but necessary, for many individuals with ED-PTSD.

Large nationally representative studies suggest that approximately 20% of people with EDs also have current posttraumatic stress disorder (PTSD; Dansky et al., 1997; Hudson et al., 2007). Prevalence rates are higher in ED treatment-seeking samples, with the highest rates (approximately 50%) documented in intensive treatment settings (Gleaves et al., 1998; Trottier, 2020; Vanzhula et al., 2019). ED symptoms such as binge eating, self-induced vomiting, and severe food restriction/underweight appear to be ways that people with ED-PTSD avoid thinking about, and feeling emotions related to traumatic experiences. These ED symptoms also have the potential to temper the hyperarousal symptoms of PTSD. PTSD symptoms such as intrusive memories, and strong negative feelings related to trauma are highly distressing, and avoidant coping strategies are characteristic of the disorder. Unfortunately, any degree of successful avoidance and escape from PTSD symptoms via ED symptoms is highly reinforcing and would have the consequence of perpetuating both disorders. Avoidance perpetuates PTSD by preventing the individual from accepting the reality of the traumatic event, processing their natural emotions about it, and working through its meaning.

Research documenting the functional interconnections between ED and PTSD symptoms and psychopathology is emerging. Karr and colleagues found that, among individuals with ED-PTSD, purging behavior was preceded by a faster rise in negative affect and was succeeded by a faster decline in negative affect, as well as a faster increase in positive affect, compared to those without co-occurring PTSD (Karr et al., 2013). Vanzhula and colleagues identified illness pathways between PTSD intrusive symptoms (i.e., distressing dreams) and body image concerns, as well as between PTSD hyperarousal symptoms and binge eating, using network analysis (Vanzhula et al., 2019). Research methods have also been used to investigate both patient and clinician perceptions of the relationship between ED and co-occurring PTSD. A study utilizing perceived causal relations scaling found that both men and women with symptoms of ED-PTSD viewed their PTSD symptoms as being causally related to their ED symptoms (Thornley et al., 2016). In a survey study, frontline clinicians providing ED treatment strongly endorsed the notion that trauma-related symptoms are an obstacle to providing successful ED treatment and 88.5% of the clinician respondents reported that concurrent treatment for ED and PTSD is the most appropriate approach for these individuals (Trottier, Monson, Wonderlich, MacDonald et al., 2017)—yet until recently, no protocol had been developed and systematically evaluated. We initiated *PROJECT RECOVER: Overcoming Co-occurring Eating Disorders and Posttraumatic Stress Disorder through Integrated Treatment* in 2013, recognizing that PTSD is a powerful ED maintaining factor for a significant subgroup of individuals, and that a concurrent integrated treatment approach is needed to enable these individuals to recover from their ED and PTSD (Trottier et al., 2016).

The first PROJECT RECOVER treatment protocol involved concurrent delivery of an earlier version of the Cognitive Processing Therapy (CPT) for PTSD manual (P.A. Resick et al., 2010) to individuals receiving ED treatment at University Health Network (UHN) in Toronto, Canada. CPT was started after an initial period of nutritional stabilization, symptom interruption, and weight restoration (as indicated). The period of ED treatment before starting CPT was not defined, with patients receiving concurrent CPT at various stages of ED treatment in the program (cognitive-behavioral therapy [CBT]-based inpatient, day hospital, or outpatient follow-up). Subsequently, we developed and began the process of evaluating an integrated ED-PTSD treatment protocol that involves delivery of a manualized individual CBT addressing both ED and PTSD (Integrated CBT for ED-PTSD; Trottier & Monson, 2014) following a period of initial ED treatment focused on regular eating and symptom interruption.

In this paper, we describe the Integrated CBT for ED-PTSD protocol and how interventions from both CBT for ED and CPT for PTSD are utilized to address the functional relationship between ED and PTSD, and promote full recovery from both disorders. These same strategies can be used when administering CPT concurrent to ED treatment (i.e., when ED and PTSD treatment interventions are administered in separate sessions or formats) and when administering CPT on its own (i.e., in the absence of ED treatment) to individuals who have both PTSD and an ED. We also review current empirical support for Integrated CBT for ED-PTSD and make recommendations for when, and when not, to deliver CPT to individuals with ED-PTSD.

Integrated CBT for ED-PTSD

Integrated CBT for ED-PTSD (Trottier & Monson, 2014) is a 16-session individual therapy delivered on an outpatient basis. It is comprised of a combination of interventions from evidence-based treatments for ED and PTSD, namely CBT-Enhanced (CBT-E) for EDs (Fairburn et al., 2008) and CPT for PTSD (P.A. Resick et al., 2014). In our research trials, the 16 sessions were delivered over a period of 14 weeks; sessions 1–8 were delivered at a frequency of twice per week, sessions 9–12 were delivered on a weekly basis, and sessions 13–14 were delivered 2 weeks apart. This session frequency was modelled after what is typical of CBTs for ED and for the most part, is consistent with recommendations for CPT. However, recent research suggests that the less time between CPT sessions, the better the PTSD outcomes (Gutner et al., 2016). Thus, we now recommend no more than 1 week between all Integrated CBT for ED-PTSD sessions.

The first three sessions of Integrated CBT for ED-PTSD are 50 minutes in length and focus on maintaining a pattern of regular eating and preventing binge and/or purge episodes, and other ED behaviors, as well as providing a rationale for integrated concurrent treatment of ED-PTSD. Integrated CBT for ED-PTSD assumes that an initial period of ED treatment has already taken place and that the individual has established a pattern of regular eating, interrupted their pattern of binge eating and/or purging, and is familiar with the skill of self-monitoring their eating and related symptoms. Thus, the content of the initial sessions of the Fairburn and colleagues CBT-E protocol (Fairburn et al., 2008; i.e., psychoeducation about EDs and the recovery process, implementing real-time self-monitoring of eating, establishing a pattern of eating at regular intervals, and interruption of binge eating and purging behaviors) is assumed to have already been covered and is not included in the Integrated CBT for ED-PTSD protocol. CBT-E interventions aimed at addressing maintaining mechanisms—including residual dieting, overconcern with weight or shape, as well as consolidating gains and relapse prevention, are all included in the protocol. CPT is initiated starting in session 4, and at this point, sessions are lengthened to 90 minutes to allow time to cover both the CBT-E and CPT content.

At the beginning of each CBT for ED-PTSD session, the therapist checks in with the client about their completion of both ED and PTSD practice assignments, including any difficulties they may have encountered. The client's self-monitoring records of their food intake, any eating disorder symptoms/behaviors, and related events, thoughts and feelings are also reviewed at the start of the session in order to help set the session agenda. Collaborative weighing consistent with the CBT-E protocol is done on a weekly basis alongside the review of self-monitoring records. PTSD symptoms are also monitored on a weekly basis using a self-report questionnaire (e.g., Posttraumatic Stress Disorder Checklist-5 [PCL-5]; Blevins et al., 2015) and progress is reviewed periodically with the client. Each session is organized so that CBT-E content is covered first, followed by CPT content. Within both the CBT-E and CPT content sections of each session, the therapist looks for opportunities to discuss and develop a shared understanding of how the client's ED and PTSD may be functionally connected. Below we outline how we have adapted or apply CBT-E and CPT interventions to address the functional relationship between ED and PTSD in Integrated CBT for ED-PTSD.

Integrating PTSD symptoms into the cognitive behavioral individualized formulation of ED maintenance

CBT-E involves collaboratively developing an individualized formulation of the patient's eating problem (Fairburn et al., 2008). The goal of the individualized formulation is to help engage clients in understanding how their ED is maintained, and thus, how it can be successfully treated. By jointly developing an individualized ED formulation that includes PTSD symptoms in the initial sessions of Integrated CBT for ED-PTSD, the therapist helps the patient to begin to see and understand the potential functional links between their PTSD and ED symptoms. This also helps to build a strong rationale for addressing symptoms of both disorders concurrently. In our experience, with a little reflection and encouragement, patients are able to articulate functional links between their ED and PTSD symptoms. Some clients are reluctant to reflect on the connection, because doing so involves overcoming their avoidance of thinking about the trauma that happened to them, and facing the need to both work through the traumatic experience and give up their ED behaviors, which they tend to value highly. Individuals with ED-PTSD may be particularly wedded to their ED behaviors because they not only function to help them control their body weight and/or shape, but also to attenuate their PTSD symptoms, which is highly reinforcing.

An example of a cognitive-behavioral formulation of ED maintenance adapted to include PTSD is shown in Figure 1. When creating the individualized formulation collaboratively with the patient, the patient's own words and language are used as much as possible rather than the technical and nonspecific terms used in Figure 1 (Fairburn et al., 2008). Figure 2 depicts an example of a personalized formulation of ED-PTSD maintenance. The maintenance model depicted in Figure 1 includes a potential direct functional link between PTSD-related beliefs and weight and/or shape control behaviors, as well as an indirect link via overvaluation of body weight and/or shape. PTSD-related negative emotions, intrusion symptoms, and hyperarousal have the potential to be functionally linked to both weight and/or shape control behaviors and episodes of binge eating.

The individualized ED-PTSD formulation can and should be added to and revised over the course of therapy as the therapist and patient develop a better understanding of the individual client's ED and PTSD symptoms, and how they are interconnected. Referring back to the formulation over the course of treatment can help motivate patients to make the necessary changes to move forward on the path to recovery from both PTSD and ED.

Integrating the ED into psychoeducation about PTSD maintenance

In the fourth session of Integrated CBT for ED-PTSD, CPT is initiated. The PTSD content of this session focuses on providing psychoeducation about what PTSD is, how someone (and the patient in particular) can get "stuck" in recovering from a traumatic event, and how CPT can help them to get unstuck and facilitate recovery from their PTSD. The psychoeducation emphasizes the role that avoidance plays in maintaining PTSD symptoms, as well as the role of emotions and cognitions related to the trauma. The potential for a functional relationship between PTSD symptoms and ED

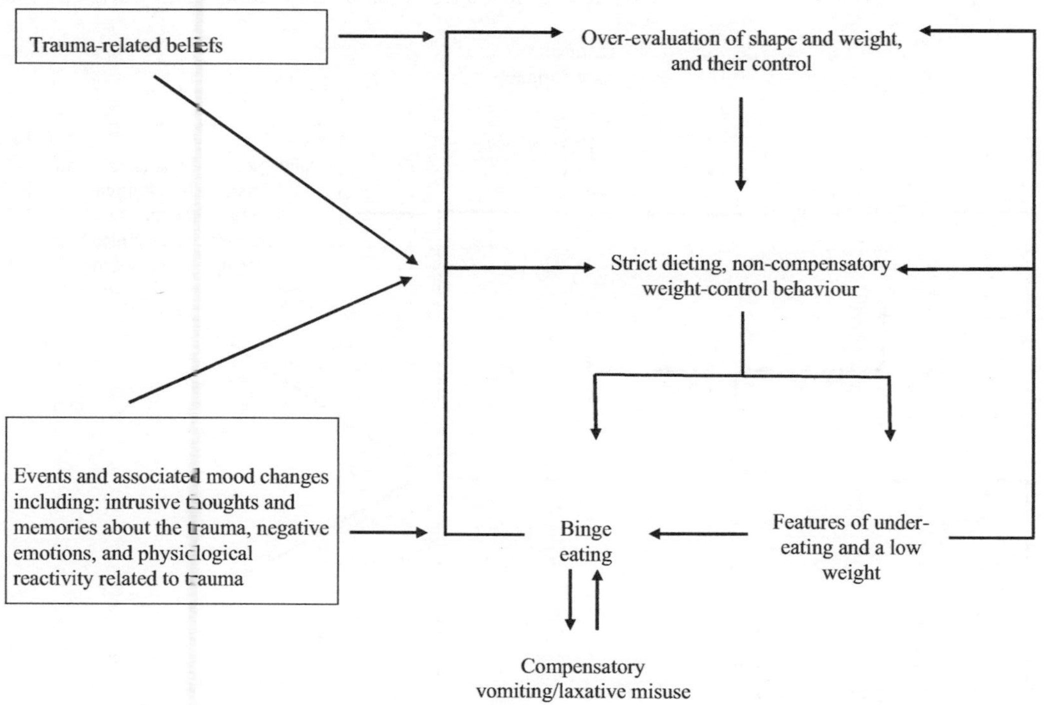

Figure 1. Cognitive-Behavioral formulation of co-occurring eating disorder and posttraumatic stress disorder. Adapted from Fairburn et al. (2008). In C.G. Fairburn (Ed). *Cognitive behavior therapy and eating disorders* (pp.47–196). The guilford press.

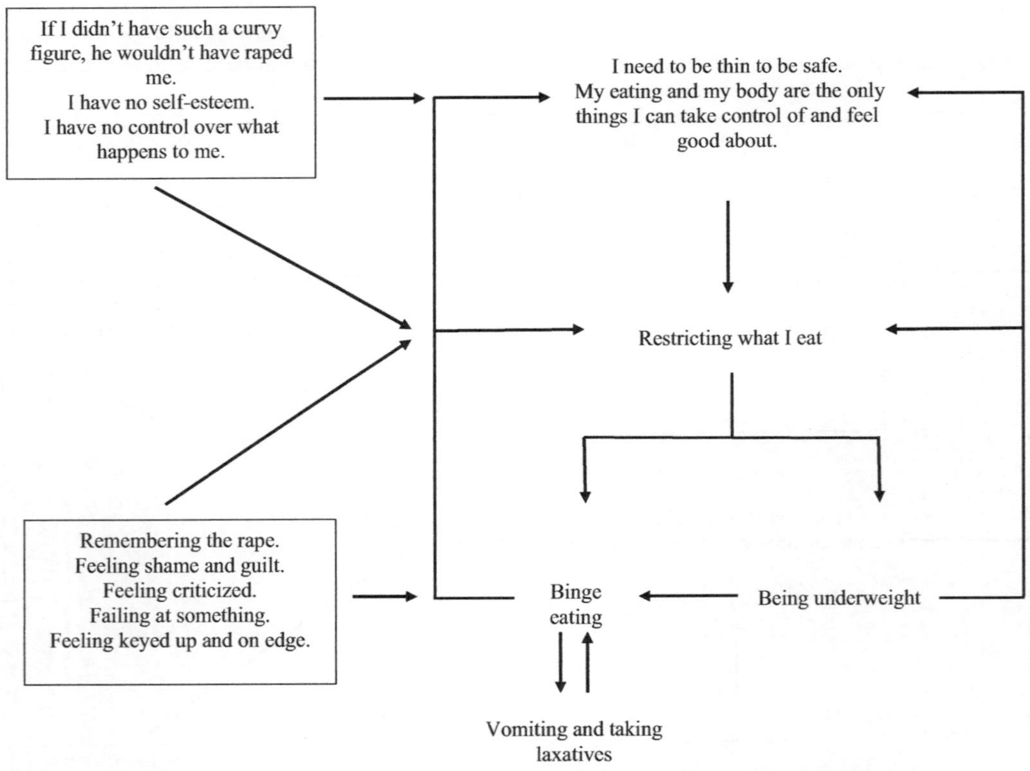

Figure 2. Personalized cognitive-behavioral formulation of co-occurring eating disorder and posttraumatic stress disorder. Adapted from Fairburn et al. (2008). In C. G. Fairburn (Ed). *Cognitive behavior therapy and eating disorders* (pp.47–196). The Guilford Press.

behaviors is explained. In particular, psychoeducation about how ED symptoms such as binge eating, purging, dietary restriction, excessive exercise, and underweight can be ways people avoid PTSD-related memories, thoughts and feelings is provided. All of these ED symptoms have the potential to help individuals distract, numb out from, and even forget trauma-related memories, thoughts, and feelings. They also have the potential to decrease hyperarousal symptoms of PTSD.

A significant portion of this session is spent explaining the cognitive model of PTSD and PTSD recovery. CPT is based on the premise that PTSD is maintained by maladaptive beliefs about the causes and consequences of an individual's traumatic event(s). In CPT, these maladaptive beliefs related to trauma are called "stuck points." In individuals with ED-PTSD, there is often a relationship between PTSD-related beliefs and ED behaviors. For example, the belief "I can't cope with what happened to me" often leads to using ED behaviors to distract from, numb, and overall, avoid thoughts and feelings about the trauma.

ED-PTSD stuck points

In individuals with ED-PTSD, stuck points that connect the ED to trauma and PTSD symptoms are often present and are important to identify and examine in order to address the functional relationship between them, and to facilitate both PTSD and ED recovery. Following the first session of CPT (the fourth session of Integrated CBT for ED-PTSD), patients write an Impact Statement about why they think the trauma happened to them and how it has affected their beliefs about themselves and others in the areas of safety, trust, power/control, esteem and intimacy. In Integrated CBT for ED-PTSD, patients are asked to write an additional statement about any connection they see between their ED and the trauma that happened to them. In particular, they are asked to consider how the trauma may have affected their beliefs and behaviors related to eating, body weight, and/or shape. This additional practice assignment is instrumental in elucidating stuck points that connect the trauma and/or PTSD symptoms to the ED, as well as in identifying ED behavioral patterns related to PTSD that need to be addressed in treatment. This additional practice assignment can also be used when delivering CPT to individuals with ED regardless of whether they are receiving integrated/concurrent ED treatment.

In CPT, maladaptive beliefs that are related to the cause of the traumatic event and interfere with accepting the reality of what happened (assimilated stuck points) are distinguished from overgeneralized beliefs related to the implications of the trauma (overaccommodated stuck points). Treatment focuses on resolving assimilated stuck points before overaccommodated ones. In our experience, ED-PTSD stuck points are most often overaccommodated beliefs, although they can also be assimilated ones. PTSD in individuals with ED is most frequently consequent to sexual trauma (e.g., Reyes-

Table 1. Examples of stuck points connecting trauma to an eating disorder.

Stuck Point Type
Assimilated
(1) If I didn't have large breasts, then he wouldn't have been attracted to me (and raped me).
(2) If I didn't have such a curvy body, this wouldn't have happened.
Overaccommodated
(1) I need to be underweight so that no one is attracted to me. (If I'm underweight, then I'll be safe from sexual assault.)
(2) I deserve to suffer.
(3) My body is disgusting/dirty.
(4) Controlling my eating and body is a way for me to be in control.
(5) I can't tolerate being in my body (because it reminds me of being raped/caused the rape).
(6) I need my eating disorder to cope with what happened to me.
(7) If I look sick, then I won't get beaten.
(8) I am only worthwhile if I am thin.

Rodríguez et al., 2011; Trottier, 2020), and in these cases, the individual's body often becomes a focus of self-blame (Trim et al., 2017). Curvy figures, large breasts, etc., often referred to by clients as "womanly" bodies or figures, are perceived as causal factors in the sexual assault. Body weight and/or shape can also become the focus of overgeneralized beliefs related to the trauma. Following the resolution of assimilated stuck points, CPT addresses overgeneralized beliefs related to trauma in the areas of safety, trust, power/control, esteem and intimacy. Assimilated beliefs are resolved first because they contribute to overaccommodated beliefs. Overaccommodated beliefs across all five themes can relate to self and/or others and have the potential to relate to the ED, as well as the trauma. Table 1 provides some examples of common ED-PTSD stuck points.

ED-PTSD stuck points can be effectively addressed using standard CPT techniques (Socratic dialogue and a series of cognitive behavioral worksheets). Assimilated stuck points wherein the person places blame or responsibility for a traumatic event on their body weight and/or shape (e.g., "He raped me because of my large breasts") are addressed by helping the person to recognize that when they look to themselves to explain why the traumatic event happened, they are neglecting the role that the perpetrator played in causing the traumatic event. Placing blame on one's body for a sexual assault is akin to blaming oneself for wearing a short skirt or other revealing attire. Neither is a causal link in the chain of events leading to a sexual assault. In fact, it is quite possible that the client may have still been attacked if they were not wearing a skirt or did not have large breasts. Helping them to accept the reality of the traumatic event and understand that the tendency to blame oneself for being victimized comes from a natural desire to control and prevent negative events can enable them to let go of the self-blame and instead place blame and responsibility where it belongs—on the perpetrator. Below we review how overgeneralized beliefs across each of the five themes can become connected to an ED and how these overaccomodated ED-PTSD stuck points can be effectively addressed in CPT.

Safety

Disrupted beliefs about one's ability to keep oneself safe or the dangerousness of others often become connected to body weight and/or shape in individuals who have been sexually assaulted or abused. For these individuals, being underweight (or sometimes overweight) is a safety strategy aimed at preventing future assaults or abuse (Trim et al., 2017). They believe that being underweight (or overweight) will make them unattractive or less noticeable to potential perpetrators. Victims of physical assault or domestic violence may also see being underweight and appearing frail as a way to prevent future abuse. Socratic dialogue should be used to help the client recognize and challenge their problematic beliefs about the likelihood of such an event happening again and the dangerousness of others. It is also important to help the individual recognize what behaviors or factors might increase the risk of victimization and to identify reasonable safety practices. Helping them to recognize and appreciate that the costs of being underweight are very high and that being underweight is not a reasonable way to prevent future victimization is important to recovering from both their ED and PTSD.

Trust

Many people who have PTSD, particularly PTSD related to interpersonal victimization, have difficulties trusting in themselves and others. Disrupted beliefs related to trust in others following trauma often lead to problems in interpersonal relationships and may lead to social isolation. Difficulty trusting in one's own judgment following trauma can lead to difficulties with decision-making, self-criticism, and anxiety (P. A. Resick et al., 2017). Stuck points related to trust can also perpetuate ED behaviors and psychopathology. Individuals with ED-PTSD sometimes see their ED as the only thing they can trust in their lives. These clients describe the ED as a familiar, dependable, and consistent force in their life; often referring to the ED as if it were a trusted friend. For those with ED-PTSD who struggle with trusting in their own judgment, the sense of purpose and direction the ED can provide in their day-to-day lives is comforting. In our experience, addressing trust-related stuck points (e.g., "I can't trust anyone"; "If I trust someone, they will hurt me"; "People are out to take advantage of me"; "I can't trust my own judgement") through Socratic dialogue, as well as helping clients to learn to view trust as a multidimensional construct that ideally starts out neutral and is earned (or diminished) over time, is effective at resolving these stuck points. As their view of trust shifts, the ED is no longer seen as a needed source of trust and dependability. For some, Socratic dialogue directly examining the premise that the ED is akin to a trusted friend or family member may be needed.

For individuals with ED-PTSD, difficulties with trust often arise in the context of the therapeutic relationship—particularly during ED treatment as clients find it difficult to relinquish some degree of control, and trust treatment providers' recommendations regarding food, weight, and compensatory behaviors (Trim et al., 2017). In our experience, helping clients resolve assimilated stuck points about their trauma helps to build a strong trusting therapeutic relationship that can also help to challenge trust-related stuck points, and facilitate trust in the therapist's recommendations regarding eating, weight, and their control.

Power/Control

EDs are often linked to issues of control, even in individuals without co-occurring PTSD (e.g., Froreich et al., 2017; Surgenor et al., 2002). Thus, ED-PTSD stuck points related to power and control need to be addressed to facilitate ED recovery. Individuals with ED-PTSD often struggle with feeling powerless and thinking they need to be in complete (or near complete) control. Typically, controlling eating and body weight and/or shape is a means of gaining a sense of control in one's life. Beliefs about being out of control can also contribute to episodes of binge eating. In Integrated CBT for ED-PTSD, Socratic dialogue is utilized to help clients recognize that over-controlling eating, weight and/or shape does not realistically solve the problem of feeling powerless. Highlighting the ways in which the client already exerts appropriate control in their lives and helping them identify areas where they can appropriately and effectively exert some control (e.g., asserting needs with others) is helpful in challenging stuck points about powerlessness. For those with issues of overcontrol, recognizing the ineffectiveness and costs of trying to control everything (including weight/shape/eating) through Socratic dialogue can help motivate clients to shift their beliefs.

Self-esteem

Most individuals with EDs regard themselves negatively and overvalue body weight and/or shape in judging their own self-worth. Negative self-esteem related beliefs, and beliefs linking self-esteem to weight and/or shape, in particular, may be particularly strong in individuals with ED-PTSD (Scharff et al., 2019; Trottier, 2020). In many, pursuing a thin idealized body is seen as the only way to achieve a positive sense of self, and in some, beliefs about being unworthy and/or deserving of suffering are expressed through ED behaviors such as starvation and purging. These beliefs are associated with strong negative emotions, which the ED typically functions to numb. Although overaccommodated stuck points are overgeneralized beliefs that flow from assimilated stuck points (e.g., "The trauma happened to me because I did something bad. I'm a bad person."), once established, overaccommodated stuck points can be used to seemingly confirm assimilated beliefs and contribute to assimilated appraisals in the event of future trauma (e.g., "I'm a bad person. The trauma happened to me because I'm bad."). Thus, addressing assimilated beliefs about the role of the individual's body weight/shape in their trauma is key, as well as negative overaccommodated self-esteem beliefs to prevent the re-emergence of assimilated beliefs and, ultimately, PTSD.

Overvaluing body weight and/or shape in determining self-worth is thought to be the core cognitive feature of EDs. Notably, CBT-E does not involve formal cognitive interventions. Instead, behavioral change, and analysis of the effects and implications of the behavioral changes, is seen as the most powerful means of producing change in overvaluing weight and/or shape. Nonetheless, in our experience, the CPT framework and interventions can be helpful in shifting strongly held beliefs about the importance of body weight and/or shape in individuals with ED-PTSD. We encourage our clients to identify ED stuck points (i.e., beliefs that are an obstacle to them recovering from their ED) and to work on them using the CPT worksheets. In our experience, the ED-specific stuck points identified by ED-PTSD clients are related to overvaluing body weight and/or shape and are central to the maintenance of their ED. In some cases where the client has resolved their assimilated appraisals about the trauma but continue to strongly overvalue weight and/or shape (e.g., "I am nothing unless I am thin."), we have had success with pointing out how strongly they blamed themselves for the trauma at the start of treatment, and how, through CPT, they changed their mind about the cause of the traumatic event. This has typically led to a willingness to work on their ED stuck points with the CPT worksheets, and in some individuals has led to a major shift in insight into their ability to choose to experiment with different ways of thinking about the importance of body weight and/or shape. One caveat is that it is important that clients do not work on their ED-specific stuck points in place of their trauma-related stuck points. We stress the importance of doing at least one worksheet related to the trauma on a daily basis and any additional worksheets on the trauma or ED are a bonus.

Self-intimacy

In CPT, self-intimacy refers to one's ability to cope and to comfort oneself appropriately, as well as developing an understanding of one's values and preferences separate from PTSD (and in ED-PTSD, the ED as well). It is well known that EDs are related to emotion dysregulation and efforts to soothe, change, or cope with difficult emotions (Brockmeyer et al., 2012; Smyth et al., 2007). Symptoms of PTSD include intense and prolonged psychological distress in response to reminders of trauma, a persistently negative emotional state, and inability to experience positive emotions. Unfortunately, ED behaviors have the potential to temper these highly distressing emotional states, at least in the short term (Karr et al., 2013) and individuals with ED-PTSD often report that ED behaviors and symptoms such as binge eating, purging and being underweight help reduce the intensity and frequency of PTSD intrusion symptoms. Stuck points such as "I need my ED to cope with what happened to me" are common in ED-PTSD. Individuals who experienced a trauma that involved their bodies being violated such as rape, sexual assault, physical assault or abuse, often experience their bodies as strong reminders of the trauma, and have beliefs such as "I can't tolerate being in my body". At this point in treatment (intimacy is the last theme that is addressed), clients have usually gathered a good deal of evidence that they can, in fact, cope with the trauma that happened to them without their ED behaviors; in many cases, this evidence will have already shifted their beliefs about their ability to cope with what happened. Others will need to practice examining their stuck points about coping without the ED through the use of the CPT worksheets.

Although many people with longstanding mental health problems, including PTSD, may express a fear of not knowing who they are without their illness, in our experience, this fear is highly prevalent and strong in individuals with EDs. EDs are unique in that the disorder itself tends to be highly valued because of the importance that is placed on eating, weight and/or shape, and because of the psychological functions EDs can serve (Vitousek & Hollon, 1998). Stuck points that interfere with the client returning to a developmentally appropriate level of functioning are important to identify and address. Encouraging clients to engage in worthwhile and enjoyable activities is often helpful for a number of reasons including that these activities can be used as strategies to interrupt patterns of negative thinking and problematic behaviors, and helping clients to begin to come to an understanding of who they are without their ED and PTSD. The idea of building an identity separate from their ED and PTSD is often overwhelming to individuals with ED-PTSD, and psychoeducation explaining that the process can start with identifying their preferences, interests, and values can help to demystify the process and make it feel more manageable.

Empirical support

In our first uncontrolled study, Integrated CBT for ED-PTSD (Trottier & Monson, 2014) was delivered to 10 individuals following a course of intensive ED treatment (inpatient and/or day hospital treatment) in the ED Program at UHN (Trottier, Monson, Wonderlich, Olmsted et al., 2017). There were statistically significant and large magnitude improvements in PTSD, depression, and anxiety over the course of Integrated CBT for ED-PTSD. Approximately 90% of the individuals who were remitted from behavioral ED symptoms at the end of intensive treatment and the start of Integrated CBT for ED-PTSD remained remitted from their ED behaviors, and also remitted from their PTSD over the course of Integrated CBT for ED-PTSD. These results were encouraging and led to the design of an initial randomized controlled trial (RCT) comparing Integrated CBT for ED-PTSD to CBT for ED only following a course of intensive ED treatment. The goal of this initial RCT was to determine whether Integrated

CBT for ED-PTSD was superior to CBT for ED alone in improving PTSD symptom severity. Number and length of therapy sessions were controlled for such that participants who did not receive integrated CPT received additional time spent on CBT-E interventions. Preliminary analyses of all available pre- and post-treatment data indicated that Integrated CBT for ED-PTSD resulted in significantly lower PTSD symptom severity at post-treatment compared with CBT for ED alone (Trottier et al., 2019).

Of note, the integrated treatment in both the initial uncontrolled trial and RCT was based on earlier versions of the CPT manual (P.A. Resick et al., 2014). Thus, consistent with the manuals at the times the studies were initiated, Integrated CBT for ED-PTSD involved written accounts of the trauma memory in both trials. The current version of the CPT manual (P. A. Resick et al., 2017) does not include written accounts as part of the standard protocol. However, the manual recommends the addition of written accounts for individuals who are highly dissociative. We are currently in the process of evaluating the effectiveness of CPT delivered concurrently to intensive ED treatment. In this study, participants receive a course of CPT as an adjunct to inpatient and/or day hospital ED treatment. CPT is being delivered by ED program therapists consistent with the current CPT manual (i.e., without written accounts). Although in this protocol the individual therapy sessions contain CPT content only (i.e., no CBT-E interventions) and ED treatment is inpatient and/or day hospital treatment as usual, therapists attend to the potential functional links between the ED and PTSD as outlined above.

When to start, and consider stopping, CPT in individuals with ED

To date, and in the context of providing integrated concurrent treatment for both the ED and PTSD, we have initiated CPT after a period of nutritional stabilization, symptom interruption, and weight restoration (as needed). In both the initial uncontrolled trial and RCT of Integrated CBT for ED-PTSD, participants received at least 6 weeks of intensive CBT-based ED treatment and reached a body mass index (kg/m^2; BMI) of at least 18.5 before starting treatment. In this sense, integrated treatment has started with an initial stage or period of ED treatment to stabilize people nutritionally. It is important to note that we have not required that clients be fully abstinent from ED behaviors such as binge eating and/or purging or that they are fully weight restored before starting CBT for ED-PTSD or CPT concurrent with ED treatment. Also, we have successfully initiated CPT concurrent with intensive ED treatment after a briefer period of nutritional stabilization and at a BMI as low as 15. However, the individual was engaged in inpatient ED treatment that involved eating an adequate amount to meet their nutritional needs.

To date, we have delivered CPT within a tertiary care intensive ED treatment program aimed at individuals with moderately to extremely severe EDs.

Low weight and frequent binge eating and purging are associated with significant medical risks, as well as difficulties with concentration and cognition. Indeed, EDs are associated with elevated mortality—with anorexia nervosa having the highest mortality rate of all mental health disorders (Arcelus et al., 2011). Given this, it is reasonable to assume that people with severe to extreme severity ED require a period of nutritional restoration before being able to benefit from a trauma-focused psychotherapy. That said, at what minimum ED severity threshold this is required, and how long of a period of initial ED treatment is needed, remains an unanswered empirical question, and we have no doubt that people with ED-PTSD have been successfully treated with CPT without an initial period of ED treatment. Until we are able to answer this question based on empirical data, we encourage clinicians planning to initiate CPT with an individual with ED-PTSD to consider whether the person is nourished enough to be able to engage in the cognitive and emotional processing that is integral to CPT before starting treatment.

Regardless of whether CPT is being provided in the context of integrated/concurrent ED treatment, we currently recommend at least a 1-month pattern of regular eating before initiating CPT in individuals with ED-PTSD who are engaging in significant food restriction. Caution should be exercised in initiating CPT in individuals who are underweight—however, we do believe CPT can be effectively administered to those at low BMIs who have undergone a period of nutritional stabilization and are currently meeting their full nutritional requirements. The risk in starting CPT with someone who is significantly underweight and not meeting their nutritional needs is that their cognitive functioning and ability to feel and express emotions may be significantly hindered by the effects of starvation—and both of these factors are important to the therapeutic process of CPT. Another concern is that for individuals who are actively engaging in a pattern of eating disorder behaviors such as food restriction, binge eating, purging, or excessive exercise, these behaviors are likely to function, at least in part, as avoidant coping strategies that may interfere with recovery from PTSD. If a client is attending sessions and doing their practice assignments but is coping with difficult thoughts and feelings through bingeing and purging, for example, CPT may not be effective due to continued reliance on avoidant coping strategies that maintain PTSD. Carefully considering these issues before initiating CPT with an individual with ED-PTSD is likely to decrease the risk of the ED interfering with the effectiveness of CPT for the individual. That said, it is still important to monitor the frequency and severity of ED symptoms over the course of CPT. This can be done via self-report questionnaire at the start of each session or alternatively, clients can be asked verbally about the frequency and severity of any ED symptoms. We also regularly discuss with the client whether they may be using ED behaviors as a way of avoiding or coping with trauma-related thoughts and feelings, and to assess whether this may be interfering with the effectiveness of CPT for the individual. Finally, it is also important to have a process for monitoring body weight and/or BMI in those who are underweight or at risk of losing weight over the course of CPT. If a client with ED-PTSD is actively participating in CPT and appears to be benefiting (based on reductions in PTSD symptoms assessed via self-report questionnaire [e.g., PCL-5]), then we are inclined to continue with CPT even if there is a worsening of ED symptoms. However, CPT should be put on hold if the individual's ED severity increases to the point that they cannot do their practice assignments effectively or they become medically unstable. If PTSD symptoms are not improving as expected, and an individual is engaging in significant ED symptoms/is significantly underweight, then we recommend stopping CPT and referring the individual for ED treatment. The individual can then return to CPT once they have made adequate improvements to their ED symptoms, or if available, could receive a course of integrated/concurrent treatment for ED and PTSD. We also encourage clinicians providing ED treatment (without concurrent PTSD treatment) to individuals with co-occurring PTSD, to consider whether PTSD may be an ED maintaining mechanism for the individual and to discuss potential functional links with their client and to recommend and refer them for evidence-based PTSD treatment to prevent ED relapse and facilitate long-term recovery. We believe that integrated/concurrent treatment for both the ED and PTSD affords the best opportunity to address these functional relationships between the two disorders and to prevent having to interrupt PTSD treatment due to the worsening of ED symptoms and to maximize the effectiveness of CPT for these individuals.

Conclusion

We are still in the early stages of evaluating Integrated CBT for ED-PTSD (Trottier & Monson, 2014) and other protocols for concurrent integrated delivery of CPT to individuals receiving ED treatment, and it is not yet known whether integrated concurrent treatment is superior to pure sequential treatment (e.g., CBT for ED followed by CPT). Nonetheless, in our experience, few individuals with ED-PTSD who present for ED treatment have sought out trauma-focused treatment (and the few that have are extremely unlikely to have received an evidence-based PTSD treatment), and many are not even aware that they have symptoms of PTSD. When these individuals present for ED treatment, it is an important opportunity to assess them for PTSD, engage them about their PTSD symptoms, and ultimately provide efficacious PTSD treatment that they otherwise would not receive. Given the existing evidence that a substantial portion of those who receive the best available treatment for ED do not have a good response (Hay, 2013), combined with evidence of strong associations between trauma, PTSD, and EDs (e.g., Molendijk et al., 2017), as well as clinician and patient perceptions about the bidirectional and functional relationship between ED and trauma-related symptoms (Thornley et al., 2016; Trottier et al., 2017a), there is good reason to believe that integrated concurrent treatment of ED-PTSD will be not only beneficial, but necessary, for many individuals with ED-PTSD. Our experience suggests that CPT can be successfully integrated with ED treatment and CBT-E interventions, in particular.

Acknowledgments

We are grateful to Drs. Traci McFarlane, Michelle Mahan, and Danielle MacDonald for their ongoing work delivering the interventions described in this paper, and for their invaluable insights. We are also grateful to Ms. Madeleine Weichel for her assistance with manuscript preparation.

Funding

This work was supported by an Academic Scholar's Award awarded by the Department of Psychiatry, the University of Toronto to the first author.

References

Arcelus, J., Mitchell, A. J., Wales, J., & Nielsen, S. (2011). Mortality rates in patients with anorexia nervosa and other eating disorders: A meta-analysis of 36 studies. *Archives of General Psychiatry*, *68*(7), 724–731. https://doi.org/10.1001/archgenpsychiatry.2011.74

Blevins, C. A., Weathers, F. W., Davis, M. T., Witte, T. K., & Domino, J. L. (2015). The posttraumatic stress disorder checklist for DSM-5 (PCL-5): Development and initial psychometric evaluation. *Journal of Traumatic Stress*, *28*(6), 489–498. https://doi.org/10.1002/jts.22059

Brockmeyer, T., Holtforth, M. G., Bents, H., Kämmerer, A., Herzog, W., & Friederich, H. (2012). Starvation and emotion regulation in anorexia nervosa. *Comprehensive Psychiatry*, *53*(5), 496–501. https://doi.org/10.1016/j.comppsych.2011.09.003

Dansky, B. S., Brewerton, T. D., Kilpatrick, D. G., & O'Neil, P. M. (1997). The national women's study: Relationship of victimization and posttraumatic stress disorder to bulimia nervosa. *International Journal of Eating Disorders*, *21*(3), 213–228. https://doi.org/10.1002/(sici)1098-108x(199704)21:3<213::aid-eat2>3.0.co;2-n

Fairburn, C. G., Cooper, F., Shafran, R., Bohn, K., Hawker, D. M., Murphy, R., & Straebler, S. (2008). *Cognitive behavior therapy and eating disorders*. C. G. Fairburn Ed, 47–196. The Guilford Press.

Froreich, F. V., Vartanian, L. R., Zawadzki, M. J., Grisham, J. R., & Touyz, S. W. (2017). Psychological need satisfaction, control, and disordered eating. *British Journal of Clinical Psychology*, *56*(1), 53–68. https://doi.org/10.1111/bjc.12120

Gleaves, D. H., Eberenz, K. P., & May, M. C. (1998). Scope and significance of posttraumatic symptomatology among women hospitalized for an eating disorder. *International Journal of Eating Disorders*, *24*(2), 147–156. https://doi.org/10.1002/(sici)1098-108x(199809)24:2<147::aid-eat4>3.0.co;2-e

Gutner, C. A., Suvak, M. K., Sloan, D. M., & Resick, P. A. (2016). Does timing matter? Examining the impact of session timing on outcome. *Journal of Consulting and Clinical Psychology*, *84*(12), 1108–1115. https://doi.org/10.1037/ccp0000120

Hay, P. (2013). A systematic review of evidence for psychological treatments in eating disorders: 2005-2012. *International Journal of Eating Disorders, 46*(5), 462–469. https://doi.org/10.1002/eat.22103

Hudson, J. I., Hiripi, E., Pope, H. G., & Kessler, R. C. (2007). The prevalence and correlates of eating disorders in the National Comorbidity Survey Replication. *Biological Psychiatry, 61*(3), 348–358. https://doi.org/10.1016/j.biopsych.2006.03.040

Karr, T. M., Crosby, R. D., Cao, L., Engel, S. G., Mitchell, J. E., Simonich, H., & Wonderlich, S. A. (2013). Posttraumatic stress disorder as a moderator of the association between negative affect and bulimic symptoms: An ecological momentary assessment study. *Comprehensive Psychiatry, 54*(1), 61–69. https://doi.org/10.1016/j.comppsych.2012.05.011

Molendijk, M. L., Hoek, H. W., Brewerton, T. D., & Elzinga, B. M. (2017). Childhood maltreatment and eating disorder pathology: A systematic review and dose-response meta-analysis. *Psychological Medicine, 47*(8), 1402–1416. https://doi.org/10.1017/S0033291716003561

Resick, P. A., Monson, C. M., & Chard, K. M. (2010; 2014). *Cognitive processing therapy: Veteran/military version.* Department of Veterans' Affairs.

Resick, P. A., Monson, C. M., & Chard, K. M. (2017). *Cognitive processing therapy for PTSD: A comprehensive manual.* Guilford Publications.

Reyes-Rodríguez, M. L., Von Holle, A., Ulman, T. F., Thornton, L. M., Klump, K. L., Brandt, H., . . . Bulik, C. M. (2011). Posttraumatic stress disorder in anorexia nervosa. *Psychosomatic Medicine, 73*(6), 491–497. https://doi.org/10.1097/PSY.0b013e31822232bb

Scharff, A., Ortiz, S. N., Forrest, L. N., & Smith, A. R. (2021). Comparing the clinical presentation of eating disorder patients with and without trauma history and/or comorbid PTSD. *Eating Disorders*, 29(1), 88-102. https://doi.org/10.1080/10640266.2019.1642035

Smyth, J. M., Wonderlich, S. A., Heron, K. E., Sliwinski, M. J., Crosby, R. D., Mitchell, J. E., & Engel, S. G. (2007). Daily and momentary mood and stress are associated with binge eating and vomiting in bulimia nervosa patients in the natural environment. *Journal of Consulting and Clinical Psychology, 75*(4), 629–638. https://doi.org/10.1037/0022-006X.75.4.629

Surgenor, L. J., Horn, J., Plumridge, E. W., & Hudson, S. M. (2002). Anorexia nervosa and psychological control: A reexamination of selected theoretical accounts. *European Eating Disorders Review, 10*(2), 85–101. https://doi.org/10.1002/erv.457

Thornley, E., Vorstenbosch, V., & Frewen, P. (2016). Gender differences in perceived causal relations between trauma-related symptoms and eating disorders in online community and inpatient samples. *Traumatology, 22*(3), 222–232. https://doi.org/10.1037/trm0000071

Trim, J. G., Galovski, T., Wagner, A., & Brewerton, T. D. (2017). Treating eating disorder—PTSD patients: A synthesis of the literature and new treatment directions. In *Clinical handbook of complex and atypical eating disorders* (pp. 40–59). Oxford University Press.

Trottier, K. (2020). Posttraumatic stress disorder predicts non-completion of day hospital treatment for bulimia nervosa and other specified feeding/eating disorder *European Eating Disorders Review, 28(3), 343-350.*

Trottier, K., & Monson, C. M. (2014). *Integrated cognitive behavioral therapy for co-occurring eating disorder and posttraumatic stress disorder.* Unpublished manual.

Trottier, K., Monson, C. M., Wonderlich, S., Cao, L., & Crosby, R. (2019). Project Recover: Results of a first randomized controlled trial of integrated CBT for co-occurring eating disorder and posttraumatic stress disorder. *Presented at the annual meeting of the Eating Disorder Research Society*, Chicago, Illinois.

Trottier, K., Monson, C. M., Wonderlich, S. A., MacDonald, D. E., & Olmsted, M. P. (2017). Frontline clinicians' perspectives on and utilization of trauma-focused therapy with individuals with eating disorders. *Eating Disorders*, *25*(1), 22–36. https://doi.org/10.1080/10640266.2016.1207456

Trottier, K., Monson, C. M., Wonderlich, S. A., & Olmsted, M. P. (2017). Initial findings from Project Recover: Overcoming co-occurring eating disorders and posttraumatic stress disorder through integrated treatment. *Journal of Traumatic Stress*, *30*(2), 173–177. https://doi.org/10.1002/jts.22176

Trottier, K., Wonderlich, S. A., Monson, C. M., Crosby, R. D., & Olmsted, M. P. (2016). Investigating posttraumatic stress disorder as a psychological maintaining factor of eating disorders: Eating disorders and posttraumatic stress disorder. *International Journal of Eating Disorders*, *49*(5), 455–457. https://doi.org/10.1002/eat.22516

Vanzhula, I. A., Calebs, B., Fewell, L., & Levinson, C. A. (2019). Illness pathways between eating disorder and post-traumatic stress disorder symptoms: Understanding comorbidity with network analysis. *European Eating Disorders Review*, *27*(2), 147–160. https://doi.org/10.1002/erv.2634

Vitousek, K., Watson, S., & Wilson, G. T. (1998). Enhancing motivation for change in treatment-resistant eating disorders. *Clinical Psychology Review*, *18*(4), 391–420. https://doi.org/10.1016/s0272-7358(98)00012-9

Index

Note: **Bold** page numbers refer to tables and *italic* page numbers refer to figures.